HAVE GRANDCHILDREN, WILL TRAVEL

the hows and wheres
of a glorious vacation
with your
children's children

by
VIRGINIA SMITH SPURLOCK

pilot books . . . *guides to the good life, all your life*

PILOT BOOKS
127 Sterling Avenue
Greenport, New York 11944

Library of Congress Cataloging in Publication Data

Spurlock, Virginia 1926-
Have Grandchildren, Will Travel: the hows and wheres of a glorious vacation with your children's children / by Virginia Smith Spurlock
p. cm. -- (The well-prepared traveler series)
ISBN 0-87576-212-3 (alk. paper)
1. United States--Guidebooks. 2. Family recreation--United States--Guidebooks. 3. Grandchildren--Travel--United States--Guidebooks.
I. Title. II. Series.
E158.S76 1997
917.304'929--dc21 97-27405
CIP

Printed in the United States of America

ABOUT THE AUTHOR

Virginia Smith Spurlock is a psychologist, author, world-traveler and devoted grandmother of five grandchildren. In addition to "Have Grandchildren, Will Travel", she has written articles for many publications and co-authored "Cruising Canada by Car...Good Times on a Budget" which is also available from Pilot Books.

Since the death of her husband Charles, she has continued to live and write in Nashville and Clifton, Tennessee and remains an ardent traveler, with and without grandchildren.

To my beloved late husband,
my children and children-in-law,
without whom there would be no grandchildren,
and to my wonderful grandchildren,
without whom there would be no book.

TABLE OF CONTENTS

CHAPTER

1

INTRODUCTION

Assuming you are not nearly ready for a rocking chair, gung-ho to hit the road and genuinely love being with your grandchildren, you're probably an ideal candidate for this great adventure. Remember though, that, when taking grandchildren on vacation, there's more involved than simply packing a suitcase, picking up the kids and hopping in the car. It takes a great deal of planning and preparation to make any trip special ...and that's especially true of inter-generational vacations. I hope this book will make things easier and pave the way for many wonderful trips.

THE FIRST TIME IS THE HARDEST.

Shortly before my husband's death, Stephanie, our seven year-old granddaughter, expressed a fervent desire to see the

White House. We promised to take her there during her next summer vacation. When I was suddenly widowed, I asked myself if I were brave enough to undertake such a venture alone. No question that she wanted to go and so did I but...

I discussed it with my son and his ex-wife. Without hesitation, each gave me a fervent 'go ahead'. That boosted my self-confidence. The first thing I did was buy a cellular phone for the car in case of an emergency. Then I sat down with Stephanie to pour over maps and tour books.

Our week in Washington was fantastic. Since then I have become totally addicted to traveling with my grandchildren ...and they are equally enthusiastic. We have toured, cruised, shared experiences unique to us and in so doing, established close, long-term relationships.

CHAPTER

2

GET READY!

WHERE TO START?

Start by getting the go-ahead from the parents. This must be done even before mentioning the possibility of a trip to your grandchild. In case the parent(s) give a thumbs down to the idea, it won't cast them in the role of the bad guys in the eyes of their child. Now let's say, for example, that there isn't a definite 'no' but you sense reticence on the part of one or both parents to allow their child to be carried away on an adventure over which they have little control. Go easy. No hurt feelings, no pouting. Keep a smile on your face and let it drop (at least for the time being). It will soon be time to put plan B into action.

Plan B is to invite the reticent parent and your grandchild on a day's outing. Do something you think both parent and child (especially parent) will particularly enjoy. You plan it, you execute it, you pay for it. If it's a memorable day then, some time later, ease the inter-generational vacation idea into the conversation again and reassess the reaction. If it's still negative, I suggest you forget it and satisfy yourself with one-day excursions with your grandchild—at least for the time being.

Assuming the scenario doesn't happen or your Plan B does the trick, you now have the sanction of Mom and Dad. Great. But you may have to make some tough decisions. The first one is probably the most important.

HOW OLD IS OLD ENOUGH?

Of course it depends on the maturity of the individual child. But you'll probably find (as we did) that a minimum age of 4 is a good rule of thumb. Along with that rule comes a promise to the younger ones that their time will come. Special day excursions or overnights at Granny and Grandpa's house were planned for the small fry left behind.

A situation may arise where there is a grandchild who won't want to go and who, regardless of chronological age, isn't ready to leave Mom, Dad and home. Fine. Be sure to remember him or her with something special if you travel with a brother, sister or cousin. Chances are the child will be ready next year.

On the other hand, there may be a child who *you* know isn't ready (even if he and his parents think he is). In this case the overnight trial run discussed later in this chapter is even more essential. Try to be as objective as possible when assessing your chances of success on a longer vacation. Miracles happen and a child who seems hopelessly unready for a long trip away may turn out to be the best traveling companion ever. But if homesickness is potent, he or she probably won't be able to handle the trip - now. It's kinder to promise another try next year and a lovely gift when you return from your trip to ease the disappointment.

ONE GRANDCHILD...TWO? ALL OF THEM?

Next decision. If you have more than one grandchild, you must decide whether to take one, two or more of them because, chances are, when a trip is mentioned, all your grandchildren from age two up will line up to go. Obviously, you'll give them all a turn in a way that's fair and appropriate. We don't have to tell you how to do that, you love them all and you'll make sure they're okay about who goes and when. But the guidelines we evolved over the years will help you decide how many to take on each vacation.

Taking one grandchild at a time is unquestionably the easiest and most desirable option. Nothing can replace that one-on-one relationship, especially during a child's early years. So, if at all possible, do that.

If you have several grandchildren, you can still enjoy traveling with them, it just takes a little more planning. You can keep the peace by dividing your vacation-time into smaller segments (maybe keeping one vacation just for *you*). Take one child on each trip and you'll make everybody happy and be able to give and receive that all important individual attention.

If this utopian arrangement doesn't work for you, here are more guidelines to help.

When there are two grandparents, two children of compatible ages (4-7; 8-11; 12-16 yrs.) and similar interests can be accommodated, each grandparent spending some special time with each grandchild. My husband and I traveled quite a bit with more than one of our grandchildren and found great joy seeing things, both familiar and new, come alive through their young eyes. When two grandchildren are with you, there is also the advantage of their playing together, which leaves a little rest and relaxation time for the older vacationers.

With a partner, you might even consider three (maximum four) unless you opt for the more expensive cruise or dude ranch vacation where you may take as many as you can afford (or put up with). Cruises or dude ranches, which cater to children, offer a variety of activities for different ages and are the easiest, most convenient way to accommodate everybody. Yes, you will lose out on some of the one-on-one time, but you'll still have the children all to yourself —without their parents—and that makes it special. Actually, a trip of this kind can be a lot of fun for everybody, which, after all, is what a vacation is all about, isn't it? (Chapter 16 covers cruise and ranch vacations with children).

If you are a single grandparent, as I am now, or, if you are traveling without a spouse, **do not plan to take more than two children at a time.**

You may find that pre-teens or teenagers want a companion (sibling—cousin—friend) of comparable age. Be as sure as you can that they are compatible. That doesn't mean that they won't argue or even fight. If this does happen, though, it is important that you remain objective. Stay out of their disagreements unless it endangers life or limb. Ordinarily, they will settle these things quickly if left to themselves. This age group will need and want to help in the pre-trip planning. I allow each to set three priorities—things they really want to see and do at our chosen destination—and promise at least one and more if possible.

The slightly younger age group (8-10), are probably not going to be as aware of things to do and places to go, so you and their parents (if they live a distance away from you) will need to help them research the area and then make their top choices.

Your little grandchildren will likely be happy just to pack a suitcase and go. Even though you tell them what to expect, you will need to repeat this each day. Attention spans for this age group are limited.

TAKE IT ONE STEP AT A TIME.

For you grandparents who live some distance from your grandchildren and haven't had the chance to establish and maintain a good rapport with them, start simple and go easy. Visit the family for a few days before making your decision about the vacation. Become familiar with their lifestyles, schedules, their likes and dislikes. **Get to know them** and let them know you before you launch into an elaborate, long trip.

THE OVERNIGHT TRIAL RUN

If your grandchild is not yet eight—**and, again, I don't recommend vacationing with any under the age of four without their parents**—you may want to take a local overnight trial run. I suggest local because that makes it easy to contact Mom and Dad if `someone' becomes unhappy in the middle of the night. Plan some in-town activities for a couple of days then a sleep-over at a motel or hotel.

Depending on the child's age, you may want to visit a museum or take them to the zoo. Perhaps there's a children's theatre or a good movie playing. Allow plenty of swim time in the hotel swimming pool before dinner. Let the child help decide where to eat, whether it's the hotel restaurant or, perhaps, a favorite spot nearby where he seldom goes. It could be even be a pizza delivered to your room and eaten while watching a favorite TV program.

The next morning, a room service breakfast and leisurely swim before check-out time can be the perfect ending to this mini-vacation.

Remember to keep your plans flexible and easy. This is getting to know you time, a chance to determine the dynamics between you and your youngster and get a feel for what it will be like to take a longer trip together. When your time together is over, be sure to consult your grandchild as to whether he still wants to go away without his parents. Even if he were eager to go when you talked about it earlier, this trial run may be enough for him for now.

A friend of mine recently took her four year old granddaughter to nearby King's Island with less than happy results.

"It was a disaster." she reported. "Stacy wanted her mother. Nothing pleased her. I doubt that I'll try that again."

If you feel that your trial vacation was not as successful as you had hoped, don't be discouraged. It could be a situation like that of my friend when the child is simply not ready for vacationing away from Mom or Dad. Or, you may find that *you* are not ready to assume that responsibility. Chronological age is not a true measure of emotional development on either end of the spectrum.You may want to try again in a year or so or when Mom and Dad feel the youngster is ready. If it is you who feel you are not gaited to traveling with little ones any more, explain to the child and his parents that you believe shorter-term activities will be better.

If all went well on your mini-vacation and all parties decide on a longer one, four to five days will probably be long enough for your first vacation, especially if your grandchild is less than 8.

WHERE TO GO, WHAT TO DO.

Depends on the child and, perhaps more important, the age. If your grandchild is in the 4 to 6 year group, you may want to opt for the beach, either lake or sea, or perhaps the mountains. If you're wondering what you'd do with young kids at the beach when it rains for 5 days straight, you'll find that subject covered in Chapter 18: Homesickness and Other Problems.

Sightseeing is not high on a young child's priority list. Check with your travel agent about hotels which have planned children's activities. After all, you may need a little private time, too. Keep your driving days to a minimum. Long driving days require even more patience, planning and preparation.

It won't be hard to find out what your grandchild wants to do. Children of today (especially smart grandchildren like yours and mine) are worldly and knowledgeable. Even young ones know what they want to see and do. If their goal is realistic and you can live with it, try to make that the focus of the trip. Whether the activity is making a sand castle on the beach, seeing Plymouth Rock or petting a dolphin at Sea World, it deserves top priority. Remember, though, you have the last word. Consider your own interests. Do not—I repeat **—do not attempt any type of activity which you do not feel up to physically, emotionally or financially.**

Hiking the Appalachian Trail from Georgia to Maine would tax my physical capabilities, as would white water rafting down the Snake River. A week in Paris would strain my budget and I intensely dislike fishing. So I eliminate these activities early in the planning stage. I also ordinarily do not take my grandchildren to amusement parks such as the Disneys, Busch Gardens or Six Flags. I think these are more fun for immediate families. It is not my intention to replace such vacations but to supplement them with a different kind that's enjoyable for grandchildren and grandparents alike.

With your destination mutually decided upon, you and your grandchild, if possible, should visit the public library and get books relating to the area of the country you plan to visit. If you are in different parts of the country, ask your grandchild's parents to help her with the trip research. Then you and your grandchild can have telephone meetings to set priorities.

The American Automobile Association (AAA) or other auto clubs to which you might belong, can furnish you with road maps and tour books. They can help you plan your route if you wish. Travel agents, too, can supply you with appropriate brochures and general information in addition to making your reservations for you.

Don't forget to check on senior discounts. Frequently hotel or motel chains offer discounts and allow children to stay (and in some cases, eat) free when traveling with parents or grandparents.

If you are a member of the American Association of Retired People (AARP) you may be eligible for a sizeable discount when booking a hotel or motel room. American Automobile Association (AAA) members often qualify for discounts. Don't hesitate to ask for the best deal for *you.* Some of the larger hotel chains, such as the Hilton, with its Hilton HHonors program, have special senior packages with up to 50% off their hotel rooms. These hotels often offer specials for grandchildren, too. Check with your favorite chain.

Pouring over the materials and planning the things you want to do—even over the telephone—is great fun for you and your grandchild. Anticipation is almost as good as being there.

How to get there is next on your planning agenda. If your destination is a great distance away, you may want to fly into the nearest city and rent a car for visiting outlying areas. Airplane travel is always exciting, but long trips by air, as well as on the ground, can be tedious and boring if there is no advance planning. Crayons, coloring books, books to read and hand held electronic games are easy to carry on board and fun to use. Be sure to carry some chewing gum for take-offs and landings. It helps keep the sometimes painful pressure from building in children's ears.

Traveling by car is my favorite way to go. Our country is so beautiful and there are such interesting things to see and experience every few miles. It is amazing how even the youngest child will notice the changes in topography as you drive along. It lends itself to great conversations and story telling. Keep your plans flexible enough to allow stops for anything either of you want to see.

With only one grandparent-driver-entertainer, you may want to stop for a break every couple of hours to allow both of you to relax, move about a little and perhaps have a snack before driving on. If there are two drivers, plan to switch about every one and a half to two hours. This way each grandparent can play games with the grandchild while the other drives.

Inexpensive travel games are available at Toys R Us and other outlets where toys are sold. One such popular game is *Where in the World is Carmen Sandiego?* Another is Milton Bradley's *Memory*. Take your grandchild with you when you shop and he certainly will tell you what interests him. Studying the map and plotting your own course is also fun, as is reading aloud from favorite books or books about places you are going to see. You may want to make up your own games or play those which interested your children when they were little.

Storytelling, though, is probably the favorite of all youngsters regardless of age and marvelous for grandparent couples or singles.

"Tell me about my Dad when he was little." "How did Uncle Chuck fall out of the tree and break his arm?" "Were you in a real war, Grandpa?" These and a million other questions could keep you talking and your grandchild interested from North Carolina to California.

You can turn the tables, too. Let him tell you a favorite story or ask him about his friends, favorite things and fun times.

After all, getting to know each other better is a key part of this trip and the relationship you build now is the groundwork for open communication later, during those difficult teen years when it often seems nobody talks or listens to anybody.

As with any trip, be prepared. Prudence dictated my buying a cellular phone before starting out for Washington with my granddaughter. It came in very handy when we had a flat tire on the Interstate. AAA was there shortly and we were on our way quickly. I strongly recommend this for any grandparents traveling alone or with grandkids. That way you can relax and know contact with an auto club or someone else can be quickly made should an emergency arise.

Your itinerary should be flexible. The weather may be totally uncooperative, that eagerly anticipated activity disappointing. You are tired and irritable or your grandchild is. Cancel the afternoon plans and take a long, cool dip in the hotel pool. If it's raining, go to the movies or ask the hotel for a rental VCR and rent some videos. The main thing is to **never feel that any plan is etched in stone and, if one thing doesn't work out, there's always another activity.** After all a vacation is for spontaneity and fun!

ISN'T THERE AN EASIER WAY TO ENJOY A FEW DAYS WITH MY GRANDCHILD?

Sure there is. Maybe this kind of free-wheeling vacation isn't for you. You aren't comfortable driving long distances, flying into strange cities, renting cars or making reservations. You love your grandchildren, though, and you would like to show and share with them the world in which we live.

Don't despair. There are tour companies to help you accomplish similar goals without the planning, driving and other stressful activities.

Grandtravel, a division of The Ticket Counter, Chevy Chase, MD, has developed guided tours on airconditioned motor coaches throughout the United States and abroad for grandparents and grandchildren. (800) 247-7651 (in Maryland (301) 986-0790).

Rascals in Paradise of San Francisco, CA specialize in family travel and organize small group and individual trips worldwide. (415) 978-9800.

Fun Tours, Inc. out of Lincoln, NE plans at least one special grandparent-grandchild tour each year. (800) 742-7717 in NE, ID, CO,KS,SD. All other states call collect (402) 475-3956.

The Big Red Boat of Premier Cruise Lines has a variety of special family packages, some combining a cruise with a visit to Disney World, Universal Studios Sea World or Kennedy Space Center. Call your travel agent.

Elderhostel now has a variety of inter-generational programs for grandparents and grandchildren. 75 Federal St., Boston, MA 021101.

CHAPTER 3

CHAPTER

3

GET SET!

Departure time is approaching. Excitement is running high. It is time to pack and, just as important, to make and agree on rules and expectations.

No matter where you're going or how you're getting there, whether by car, plane, bus or burro, one essential thing to remember is: **pack light**. This is not always easy to do but absolutely necessary for inter-generational travel. Neither you nor your grandchild need or want to do any undue lifting or carrying. A suitcase on wheels for you and a backpack for your grandchild plus a shared tote is ideal.

Packing doesn't have to be a nightmare. A simple rule of thumb is: if you question whether you need something, leave it at home. Make a list of what to bring and stick to it.

Things to remember:

- You don't need a million pairs of underwear and socks, they can be washed and hung in the bathroom at night.
- Bring clothing which can be mix-matched.
- Darker colors do not show dirt as easily.
- Bluejeans and shorts (according to the weather) are excellent choices for boys or girls.
- Include extra tee-shirts for emergencies.
- Take one semi-dress-up outfit in case you go to the theatre or a really nice restaurant.
- A light jacket, preferably with a hood, or sweater is necessary for cool evenings.
- Don't forget a toothbrush, sleepwear, swim suit and cover-up and a favorite toy.

You and your grandchild should pack together with parental suggestions, of course. This way you won't be hearing "Where's my toothbrush?" or "I can't find my socks," every day.

Having luggage your grandchild packed herself (with a lot of help, of course), gives her a feeling of independence and teaches organization. Let her know she is responsible for her own things, including re-packing, when it is time to change locations.

In your jointly-owned tote bag, you might want to pack things you'll share such as a hair dryer, travel clock, shampoo, toothpaste, and a fever thermometer. I also include our journals, scrapbook, a small tape recorder and tapes for the child too young to write. A requirement of mine is that a daily journal be kept. It is like a private diary and need never be shared unless the author so chooses. Writing in our journals is an every-night , just-before-sleep ritual for my grandchild and me. When we are too tired, we do it the next morning before starting out. No exceptions.

If your grandchild has daily medications, you need to keep them in a separate compartment of your suitcase. Ask the parents to write out the correct dosage and keep a running record of when and how much you administered.

One vitally important item for you to have in your possession is a parental statement, signed by the parents and notarized, giving you permission to travel with your grandchild and allowing you to give permission for emergency medical treatment in case of accident or illness. You also should have a copy of the parent's medical insurance card. These are documents grandparents should have on hand any time they are in temporary custody of their grandchildren regardless of location.

Whether you are going out of the United States or not, the best kind of identification you can have is your passport. Canada, Mexico and the islands in the Caribbean do not require passports, but you must have valid ID such as a driver's license and voter registration. If your grandchild does not have a passport, carry his birth certificate and a recent photograph along with your parental permission statement.

WHO MAKES THE RULES? *YOU DO.*

Set aside some time before you leave to sit down with your grandchild and his parents and outline your expectations of the child and the rules she or he will have to follow. This is most important and no vacation adventure should begin without such an understanding. It is doubtful that you will have discipline problems if you and your grandchild are clear about limits. This doesn't have to be a deadly serious or heavyhanded discussion, just a friendly, clarifying talk so everybody knows what to expect from each other during your fast approaching vacation.

First of all, it needs to be understood up front that **it is you who always has the last word.** When you say "no", it is "no" and non-negotiable. Undoubtedly, during your time together, limits will be tried but, if you're consistent and **never say "no" if you mean "maybe"**, the child will stop testing you.

Parents need to be involved when you're establishing the rules for your trip. You don't want to allow your grandchild to do things which are strict no-nos at home. Also they need to answer some important questions. Of course you might ask the child, but then the answers might be a tad self-serving. For example, you'll want to know:

- When is bedtime? Is this flexible and, if so, how flexible?
- Are there daily routines which need to be strictly adhered to?
- Are there any allergies, food or other kinds, to watch out for?

- How much spending money will the child have and how much can he depend upon you to supplement?
- Does he swim? Does he dive? Is he allowed in the deep end of the pool? Does he use ear plugs when swimming? How about nose guards? What kind of sun screen does he use?

You and your grandchild also need to understand and agree on certain other things before you go. Very likely both of you have established customs and habits, things you really want to do each day. Now is the time to spell them out. For example, four year old Katie always wanted to sleep with her tattered baby blanket. She told me about this and I saw to it that the blanket was packed first thing each day we travelled. Grandma, on the other hand, wanted to take a 20 minute siesta every afternoon. We worked that out too. Katie turned the tv on low and watched cartoons while her grandmother snoozed ... and woke refreshed and ready for new adventures.

Let your grandchild know that plans might have to change sometimes...that, if they do, you and he or she will make new plans together. She should know that some things you both would like to do might be beyond your endurance or budget. Let her know that if you can't do something you will discuss the reasons honestly, but, when these decisions are made, they are final.

CHAPTER

4

GO!

Departure day is finally here. The car is packed, gas tank filled. You've checked twenty times and are finally sure you have all the necessary items such as cash, credit cards, travelers cheques, parental permission, identification for both of you, glasses, sun glasses, tissues, wet wipes, your senior discount cards, reservations, confirmations and any personal items you absolutely need.

You have a box or carry-on (if flying) of travel games (both electronic and manual), crayons, coloring books, books to read and your grandchild's favorite traveling toy. (My granddaughter Dianne always takes a somewhat road-weary doll who, without a whimper, has been buried in the sand, hung out to dry on a twelfth floor balcony, and dragged by an arm off and on a lot of airplanes).

While you're traveling (especially by car), it's a good idea to have a camera close by to capture some fleeting scene you'll want to remember. If you choose not to allow your grandchild to use your camera, I suggest you make one available to him. Children see things in different ways from adults and what's important to your grandchild may not be to you. Let her take pictures of what appeals to her now and, at the very least, she'll get a good laugh out of them someday.

There are several easy to use, inexpensive cameras on the market...even disposable cameras which are easy to operate and very reasonable. In addition, Kodak and others offer how-to books on photography even for young children. (The photographic industry has realized that the earlier kids learn to take pictures, the more likely they are to continue this hobby into adult life). A little camera and/or how-to book might be a Christmas or birthday gift before your trip. Or a delightful Happy Vacation present to kick off your trip.

My 6 year old grandson, Jeff, while visiting the U.S. Space Center in Huntsville, AL, took polaroid shots of the other tourists seated around an outdoor restaurant and presented his pictures to his subjects. Several parents were so enchanted with this that they took his name and address and wrote to him after they were home. One youngster even became his first-grade pen pal.

In order to preserve your grandchild's own pictures, he needs a scrapbook. These are easy to find and usually inexpensive. Let him choose one which appeals to him. This keepsake can also hold ticket stubs, autographs, picture postcards or anything else he may accumulate along the way which he wants to keep.

If your youngster has a camera, possibly a journal and a scrapbook, he really shouldn't need other souvenirs. But whenever did a child resist a gift shop? It's essential for him to know how much he can spend and to understand that, when that money is spent, there is no more. Grandparents should resist becoming bottomless wells of cash for trinkets.

My sister and her husband emphasized this strongly to their grandson before leaving for a trip across the country. On the first night out though, 7 year-old Bryan, visited the gift shop and came out with several treasures and one dollar left. They were to be gone three weeks and planned to visit places like Disneyland and Six Flags. Too bad, Bryan. The wise grandparents stuck to their guns and, even though it was a hard lesson (for all of them), there was a good result. The former spendthrift was so eager to share his misadventure with his younger cousin that he made an indelible impression. Cousin William, on his first grandparent/grandchild trip, was so struck with Bryan's sad story that he did a lot of looking and almost no buying in the gift shops. "I don't want to be like poor Bry," he often said. And he came home with only $5.00 less than he had when he left.

At last you are on your way. Goodbye kisses have been thrown. Seat belts are fastened and you are headed toward the Interstate. You have just started your monologue on what glorious sights you will see today and how much fun you are going to have when...

The first question out of your grandchild's mouth is, "How much farther is it?" and next, "Will our hotel pool have a curvy slide?"

If you don't feel your balloon of happiness deflate just a little you are a saint.

GREAT EXPECTATIONS CAN MEAN GREAT DISAPPOINTMENT.

Keep your expectations reasonable and you won't be disappointed. Your idea of what's fun and important to do on a vacation and your grandchild's will probably not be the same. Probably not even close. For example:

On what seemed an especially endless drive across Kansas with my grandson, I spotted a sign advertising an Indian Burial Ground a few miles away. We quickly decided to go, veered off the highway and drove down some dusty back roads. We finally came to an isolated farmhouse with a paved parking lot, empty except for a few Rhode Island Red chickens pecking the dry, red earth. We got out of the car and took a rather perfunctory look around. It was obvious that Chuck was not in the least interested in this archaeological find. When we got back to the parking lot, though, he had a great time chasing the chickens. Now when anyone mentions Kansas, he quips, "Oh, yeah, that's where those scaredycat chickens were."

After returning from a trip through the Great Smoky Mountains with her grandson, my cousin Julie bemoaned, "I thought John would love hiking to the top of Clingman's Dome, I did when I was his age, but all he talks about are the great peach pancakes we had in Gatlinburg.

When we returned from Washington, DC, you would have thought the only thing Stephanie saw was the pair of ruby red slippers Judy Garland wore in the *Wizard of Oz* on display at the Smithsonian. Months later, however, when she and her friend were watching the burial of Jacqeuline Kennedy Onassis on television, Stephanie's mother heard her explaining about the eternal flame at John Kennedy's grave.

The education your grandchild is getting from your travel experiences together is not always immediately obvious. But it happens, regardless of some short term memory lapses. So relax, go with the flow and remember: kids aren't interested in how educational something is or how much you enjoyed it as a child. They just want to have fun. And what's wrong with that?

Keep in mind that any family get-together requires patience, particularly when it's the young and not so young who are getting together. Remember to really listen and love each other. This vacation can be such a precious time. Going the extra mile is well worth it. The memories you make will last forever.

Now back to that first leg of your trip. If you're a single grandparent (after hearing that question signifying impending boredom), this might be the time to put in a tape of your grandchild's favorite music or story. A friend of mine tapes fairy tales to play for her grandchildren when they are in the car, whether it is going across town to ballet lessons or to a nearby mall. I've found this works well on longer trips, too.

If there are two grandparents, the non-driver might get into the back seat and play a game or two. Hopefully, you'll be well equipped with the recommended travel box. Let your grandchild select what she wants to do. Whether it's a card game, puppet show, reading aloud, Scrabble or Travel Monopoly, it should keep you and your youngster occupied for some time.

By the time you are beginning to tire of this, it'll be time for you to take the wheel and the other grandparent to take over in the back seat. If it's grandfather's turn, he may want to make up his own story, grandfathers are universally good story tellers.

The next chapters give overviews of trips to take and places to visit with your grandchildren. They're not intended to be a complete listing of good places to travel with grandchildren (almost anyplace you both like would be) but simply suggestions I hope will inspire you and which you can adapt according to your own interests and time. While I've given my experienced opinion about the appropriate ages for grandchildren to enjoy each suggested destination, you are the best judge of your youngsters' interests and maturity level. Some kids would adore a city far earlier than others, hate a state park even though they're the right age, etcetera.

The destinations I'm including are alphabetized by name and cover a range of possibilities (parks, cities, states, even an entire geographic area). I hope you'll read them all. Some places that might otherwise not appeal to you alone just may turn out to be the perfect vacation for you and your small, beloved guest(s).

Have fun!

CHAPTER

5

BOSTON

(Appropriate for boys and girls ages 10 and up)

Don't rent a car in Boston. This wonderful, exciting, historical cradle of liberty is, in my opinion, the worst city in America in which to drive. Take an airport limousine to your hotel and tour from there. You and your grandchild will be safer and happier. Don't worry about getting around. There are great trolley tours available and the MBTA (subway) is excellent.

For this trip, perhaps more than most because of its important historical significance, you will need to prepare your youngster a little. Some suggested reading which you may do together is:

"Paul Revere's Ride"—Henry Wadsworth Longfellow
"Boston's Freedom Trail"—Terry Dunnahoo

"The Bells of Freedom"—Dorothy Gilman Butters
"The Drums of April"—Charles Mergendahl

Some kids balk at reading I know, so you may want to introduce Boston in a new and unique way. "Get Ready for Boston" is a set of two CDs of lively songs, poems and stories packaged with a 76 page booklet offering lyrics and activities for visitors. Put out by WHERE magazine, it is available at Globe Corner Children's Toy and Bookstore in Boston and Tower Records and other bookstores throughout the U.S. The price is $24.95.

I suggest that you select a hotel near the Prudential Center. This central area is a pick-up point for most of the trolleys. The Back Bay Sheraton, Hilton Boston and Colonade Hotel are three which give discounts for seniors and grandchildren. There are others, so you may want to check with your travel agent.

For your first adventure in this old city, you need to take the famous Boston Duck Tour. It leaves the Prudential Center, 101 Huntington Ave., every day from April through November at 9 a.m. Because it is so popular, though, you will need to get to the point of departure about 7:00 a.m.

"No way!" My eleven year old grandson, John, complained when told how early we would have to get up. "All these historical things have been here for hundreds of years. They'll wait." "They will." I replied. "But the Ducks won't."

The Ducks are authentic, renovated World War II amphibious landing vehicles which take you on a magic journey down the Freedom Trail listening to the tour guide tell little-known stories of places which made Boston the birthplace of freedom. Soon after you pass the New England Sports Museum and veer to the left, your vehicle suddenly splashes down into the Charles River. This half boat/ half bus takes you on a cruise down river under the Longfellow Bridge and back for an unbelievable waterside view of Boston.

Even my sometimes hard-to-please grandson John was impressed by this.

I recommend that you take this tour on your first day because, not only is it great fun but it also gives you an overview of what there is for you and your grandchild to go back and visit. This is not a tour (as are most of the trolleys) where you can get off and on whenever you choose.

Before you go to your hotel room, stop by the concierge desk and ask for brochures of the Red Beantown Trolley and find out where the nearest passenger pickup is. Tickets will probably be available there at a discount. These real San Francisco style trolleys run all day long, stopping at 21 different places of interest from the Museum of Fine Arts to the U.S.S. Constitution in Charlestown. You may get off and on as many times during the day as you wish at no extra charge. If you study the map in the brochure carefully, the two of you should be able to plan a day by day itinerary that will please both generations.

The following paragraphs describe some of the places which John and I particularly enjoyed. You will, of course, create your own list.

The Paul Revere House is the oldest home built in Boston. Nearby is the Old North Church where the two lanterns were hung on April 18th, 1775 signifying to Paul Revere that the redcoats were on their way to Concord by sea. Be sure to read Longfellow's poem before you visit these sites. By the way, Paul Revere was buried in the Old Granary Burying Ground on Fremont St. along with John Hancock, Robert Paine, Samuel Adams and Mother Goose (Elizabeth Foster Goose).

The U.S.S. Constitution and the U.S.S. Constitution Museum—where visitors may load and fire a cannon, steer a square rigger at sea and command "Old Ironsides" in battle, using computer games—is a must, especially for the small set. Next door is the Bunker Hill Pavilion where an automation of the Battle of Bunker Hill is presented in a "sound in the round" amphitheater.

On Wednesdays at 10 a.m. at the Globe Corner Bookstore, at School and Washington Sts., kids 8 years old and up, accompanied by an adult, may visit with old Benjamin Franklin (portrayed, of course, by an actor) and listen for two hours to the stories of his childhood. Admission is $10. Call 523-6658 for reservations.

Boston by Little Feet is a special hour-long volunteer guided walking tour for children ages 6 through 12. Call 367-8345 for more information.

Don't miss the New England Aquarium, a fabulous aquatic zoo where more than 70 exhibits feature sea turtles, eels, sharks and a variety of other fish which swim in what looks like a natural habitat. We especially loved the strutting penguins who inhabit a large salt water tray at the base of a tank. The Aquarium also has a whale watching boat to take you through the harbor and out to sea.

For a fun time, visit the Boston Tea Party Ship and Museum where history comes alive. You, along with the grandchildren, may participate with colonial guides in the re-enactment of the original tea party and toss chests of tea overboard. Souvenir chests of tea may be purchased there for about 19 cents.

The Childrens' Museum at 300 Congress Street contains four floors of fun for kids of all ages. There is a giant maze to climb, your youngsters could find themselves acting on TV, and there's a new exhibit called Build It! which features a construction site filled with building materials for hands on activity. Young computer whizzes or even wanna-bes will love the part called the Computer Museum. The exhibits are hands on and easy to use. There is a computer (reputed to be the largest in the world) the size of a house. In order to start it, you or your youngster will have to sit on the mouse. The gift shop here is unique, too. Ever heard of chocolate floppy discs? You can find them here—in the candy section, of course.

If either of you is a sports enthusiast, don't miss the Sports Museum of New England. It covers 22 different sports from high school to professional. My grandson came away from there happy if poorer. The museum shop is like a sports gallery with everything collectors could imagine.

While you are in the sports mood don't forget to check the Red Sox schedule. They play 17 home games in August and 12 in September at Fenway Park. The number to call is 267-1700. If there isn't a home game you might like a behind the scenes tour of the park. Times are from 10 a.m. to 1 p.m. Monday through Friday.

The age and interests of your grandchild will undoubtedly dictate the side trips you'll want to take near Boston. Check with Brush Hill Tours (a sister to the Red Beantown Trolleys) about their daily bus trips.

When it's time for lunch, if you haven't already eaten in one of the museum restaurants or the outdoor cafes which dot the streets, hop on your trolley and go to Cheers or the ever popular Hard Rock Cafe. Both are grandchildren pleasers and I don't think you will be disappointed either.

Salem is a must for your teenage grandchildren. They will revel in the witch hysteria described in the audiovisual presentation at the Salem Witch Museum. For those who have studied Nathaniel Hawthorne, don't leave Salem until you have seen his House of Seven Gables with its secret passage. It was the author's birthplace and home which he immortalized in his novel of the same name. Now a museum, it lends itself to an unforgettable visit.

If either of you would like to see where the American Revolution began, a trip to Lexington and Concord would be in order. The visitor center on the Village Green in Lexington contains a diorama of that first battle. You also can see the old bell which pealed the midnight alarm. On to

Concord to see the North Bridge and, while there, you can see where author Louisa May Alcott, Ralph Waldo Emerson and Henry David Thoreau lived and wrote.

If your grandchild is nearing college age, you certainly will want to take him or her around some of the more famous schools in the area such as Harvard, Radcliffe, Boston College and Massachusetts Institute of Technology.

Before you leave Boston be sure to take the express elevator to the 60th floor observatory of the John Hancock Tower for a panoramic view of the city which birthed a nation. See the sound and light show "Boston 1775" and be transported back in time to colonial days. Return to the present by looking down on the busy Boston Harbor, the mingling maze of one-way streets, the mix of sky scrapers and brownstones.

"Wonder how much it will be changed when I bring my grandchildren back here?" John mused half to himself as he looked out over the city.

I wonder, too.

CHAPTER

6

CALIFORNIA

(Appropriate for boys and girls ages 8 and up unless otherwise specified)

In the mind of most children, California is a fantasyland —a vivid kaleidoscope of blue skies, sun, sand, sea, snow, mountains, desert, redwoods, flowers, mansions, swimming pools, beautiful people, movies, television stars, fast cars and earthquakes. And it is a state that every child I know, from six years and up, longs to visit.

I don't for one moment suggest you try to show your grandchild the entire state. It is far too large and too diverse. Select one area (possibly two) which encompasses much that you both want to see and zero in on that.

SAN DIEGO

San Diego is a favorite city of mine, not only because of its wonderful weather and distinct Mexican flavor, but also because it's so easy to get around within it. It is a driver-friendly city with well marked streets and interstates. Most points of interest are within easy freeway access. I think the best way to see this city is by car.

If, however, you choose not to drive, a good way to see the interesting sites is to take one or more of the bus or trolley tours. Gray Line Tours offers more than 15 trips and has pick up service from most major hotels. San Diego Mini-Tours has a variety arranged bus tours including trips to Tijuana, Mexico. Old Town Trolley Tours has 2 hour bus excursions which visit BAlboa Park, Gaslamp Quarter, Seaport Village, Old Town and Coronado to name a few. You may board and re-board the trolleys at each stop. This is a good way to visit many of the places for as long as you choose and then re-board and continue on.

Since San Diego is built around a harbor, a boat tour is certainly in order. My eight year old granddaughter, Phyllis, was very taken with our cruise on the Sea Maiden where all passengers (limit of six) are allowed to take the wheel and participate in the sailing. Reservations are required. Call (619) 224-0800.

When I take a grandchild to a city on the ocean I always find it to our advantage and pleasure to find beachside accommodations. It is great fun to run in and out of the water, look for shells and participate in any other beach activities that appeal to you both. Two hotels which I have tried and like very much are the San Diego Hilton Beach and Tennis Resort near Sea World and the Ocean Park Inn on Grand Ave.

In the center of the city is an oasis of culture, beautiful Balboa Park. Here, twelve hundred acres of art galleries, restaurants, museums, theaters and quiet garden walkways make for an interesting day. It was the site of the Panama-California International Exposition in 1915-16 and many of the Spanish Renaissance exhibit halls still remain. The park's most prominent feature is the 200 ft. California Tower which contains a 100 bell carillon that chimes every 15 minutes.

World famous for its size and rarest specimens, the San Diego Zoo is tops on the visiting list for children and adults alike. It houses more than 4000 animals, many in enclosures closely resembling their natural habitats. The Hippo beach, viewed through a huge picture window, looks very much like an African marsh. Moving sidewalks take you into deep canyons, and the Skyfari aerial tramway runs from the entrance to the Horn and Hoof Mesa giving viewers a panoramic view of the Zoo. There is a double decker bus, too, which takes visitors through the maze of winding roads. I strongly suggest that you purchase the Deluxe ticket for $19.00 which includes admissions, bus and aerial tours and entrance to the Children's Zoo. You won't want to miss the latter where children have the chance to pet the more gentle of the animals and see the newborn nursery. Special live shows are presented daily at the Wegeforth Bowl and Hume

Amphitheater. The zoo opens at 9 a.m. and I recommend that you plan to arrive early and stay late. It will be a delightful day.

Carrillo National Monument on Point Loma overlooks the city and the harbor. This is an excellent vantage point for viewing the herds of gray whales as they migrate from Alaska to the Baja waters from December through February. In case you are not in San Diego at that time you can see "Baby Shamull" in a killer whale show at Sea World. Beluga whales, sea lions, dolphins and walruses, too, are included in this very enjoyable show.

The Children's Museum of San Diego (Museo de Los Ninos) is a grand, hands-on adventure. The Improv Theatre has costumes and a stage for creative drama while other creative youngsters are introduced to paint and clay.

Don't fail to take a ferry, bus or drive across to Coronado to have Sunday brunch at the historic, grand Hotel del Coronado. Even if you aren't there on a Sunday it is worth a visit and a tour.

No visit to San Diego can be complete without a bus tour across the international border to Tiuana, Mexico. Driving is not recommended because U.S. automobile insurance is not valid in Mexico. Be sure to take bottled water with you, also any snacks you think you might want. Eating and drinking in Tijuana is not a good idea. Try to select a tour to include time to see a bull fight or a jai alai game and certainly for souvenir shopping.

For the sports-minded youngster, be sure to check the game schedule for the San Diego Padres (baseball) or the Chargers (football).

If your grandchild is disappointed that he did not sample the true Mexican tacos in Tijuana, you may want to go into Old Town and try them at the Old Town Mexican Cafe and Cantina. This restaurant is on San Diego Ave. and, while you are there, you may want to take a walking tour of Old Town with its old adobe structures, quaint shops. State Park Rangers offer walking tours daily through this historic area.

Bidding farewell to this birthplace of California will not be easy. The memory of its people and its laid back charm will stay with you for a long way.

SAN FRANCISCO

(Appropriate for boys and girls 10 yrs. and up)

You don't need a car in San Francisco. Take a city bus tour, locate the places where you want to spend time and walk. The city center is small enough that you can see almost everything on foot. Certainly the hills are steep and numerous, but the cable cars run frequently if your legs just can't take another step. The fare is only $2.00.

Fisherman's Wharf is where you want to stay. From here you can get anywhere you want to go. Hotels right on the wharf are scarce but the Travelodge Hotel and the Wharf Inn are two which are perfectly located right at the wharf.

You can walk across the street from either of these hotels, catch a Tower Deluxe City tour for an overview of the city; catch the red and white Alcatraz Ferry to the "rock" from Pier 41; stroll about Pier 39 to watch the street performers and mimes; and browse through the unique little shops. Be sure to walk out on Pier 39 to watch the sea lions sunning themselves on the K dock. These marine creatures lived on the rocks below Cliff House some distance away for many years until the earthquake of 1989. After that they left the Cliff rocks and came to Pier 39 where they have made themselves at home and are under wildlife protection. Also at Pier 39 is the Citibank Cinema which shows the big screen movie, "San Francisco." Down at Pier 45 you can board the USS Pampanito, a World War II submarine. There are other old vessels which your grandchild may enjoy exploring at the Hyde St. Pier and Pier 43-2.

Your city bus tour likely will stop for a bit at Golden Gate Park. You'll love having tea in the charming tea house of the Japanese Tea Garden. And, as you ride between Hyde and Leavenworth Sts., look up Lombard St which is referred to as "the crookedest street in the world". You will believe it.

When you go to Alcatraz, be sure to take the park ranger tour. He or she will tell you stories and show you the special cells where such notorious criminals as Al Capone and the "Birdman of Alcatraz" were incarcerated. It will make your visit more interesting.

Chinatown is a city within a city. More Chinese live here than any other place outside China and Hong Kong. Walk down Grant Ave. and savor the different culture. Stop in the shops. Have tea in a tearoom. You can do this on your own or join a walking tour. The fee for the walking tour is $25.00 for adults and $10.00 for children, which I think is a little high.

Be sure to eat in the famous restaurants on Fisherman's Wharf where they say the food is as good as the view (and I agree). Encourage your grandchild to try the seafood with which he is not familiar. You may regret this as I did, however. I insisted that my granddaughter try lobster which was a first for her. She was less than eager, but did comply with my wishes. She loved it and wanted to order it at every meal while there, much to the detriment of my budget.

Do take a bus across the famous Golden Gate Bridge. You may want to take a cruise under it, too. The views are spectacular as are those on the crests of the many hills.

When your time is up in San Francisco, you may easily understand why Rudyard Kipling wrote "San Francisco has only one drawback—It is hard to leave."

LOS ANGELES

Rather than haphazardly going from one area of the city to another, decide with your grandchild the things you want to see and do before you leave home Make your hotel reservations in the general area of most of your priority attractions and, when you get to the hotel, let them arrange a rental car for you. If you need to change locations during your stay, find another hotel and go through the same procedure.

My twelve-year old granddaughter wanted to see Hollywood, the CBS and Universal studios, La Brea Tar Pits, the movie stars' homes, Mann's Chinese Theatre and the beach at Malibu, all north and west of downtown Los Angeles. We made reservations at the Hyatt Westlake in Westlake Village and found that the bus named The Great American Stage Line ran from LAX to this hotel for $15.00. After checking in, we inquired about car rental and the rental agency delivered our car to us the next morning. That night we pored over the map, decided on our route, made a few referral notes and were off early the next day. We repeated this procedure for the duration of our stay.

We drove to Burbank, where we had a tour of the NBC studios, At Warner Bros. Studios we saw the TV studios and the recording stages.

On to Beverly Hills and Hollywood, where we boarded a Gray Line sightseeing bus which took us to the Tar Pits, NBC and Paramount Studios, Mann's Chinese Theatre and a tour of the stars' homes.

We spent another entire day at Universal City and another two days on the beach at Malibu. The remainder of the week, we returned to places we'd seen on the tour but wanted to spend more time on than the tour allotted. By the end of the week we had seen all of her priorities. We did it with a maximum of planning and a minimum of effort.

Los Angeles is not the place to bring a very young grandchild. It is very helpful to have someone along who can read your notes for directions and help watch for exit signs. But it is a beautiful and exciting city and one to which you will want to return many times.

CHAPTER

7

DISTRICT OF COLUMBIA (WASHINGTON, D.C.)

(Appropriate for children ages 7 and up)

As the capitol of our nation this city should be—and is—one of the most beautiful and interesting in the world. No matter when you visit, you will find a wealth of special activities, many geared especially for the younger generation, e.g.:

- The Smithsonian Institution sponsors a Kite Festival on the Washington Monument grounds in late March or early April.
- An Easter Egg Roll takes place on the White House grounds each Easter season, usually the Monday after Easter Sunday.
- The biggest gala of all is the celebration of Independence Day on July 4th when there are parades, concerts and

special events on the Mall capped off by a huge fireworks display at the Washington Monument.

Summers in Washington are hot and humid. Spring and fall have warm days and cool nights and it can be cold and blustery in winter.

With the exception of rush hours, driving an automobile in Washington is not at all bad. The city is well planned and the streets for the most part well marked. Parking, however, is a problem and a big one. For that reason I suggest that, if you drive into the city, park the car at your hotel and leave it there. If you come in by plane, forget about renting a car. Take the limousine to the hotel.

Mass transportation is varied, excellent and sightseeing tours abound. There are bus, limousine, carriage, trolley and train tours. The Metrorail is a clean, efficient subway system which seems to interest youngsters of any age. It provides access to most of the attractions and is very economical. Maps in each station give route and fare information. Avoid using taxis if at all possible, they are very expensive.

Regardless of how you plan to get around, get a good city map and carry it with you at all times. Seeing this fine city requires walking and it is very easy to become confused and go in the wrong direction without a map. Make sure, too, that you and your grandchild wear comfortable, well broken-in shoes.

If you can, before you leave home, contact your state's senators and congressmen and get access to special services and tours of places like the White House, the Capitol and the House and Senate Buildings. This may eliminate some time-consuming (and boring) standing on line and help you see some behind the scene activities, such as Congress, if it is in session. Most children and their elders enjoy seeing our elected representatives at work. Be sure to ask for passes to the House and Senate galleries when you write.

You need to make hotel reservations well in advance of your arrival. A travel agent will assist you or, if you prefer, study the tour books and do it yourself. Nobody knows your interests and budget better than you. AAA has excellent free tour books for its members. Non-members may purchase them from the local AAA office. There is a wealth of other travel books available in the bookstores. Browse through them and find one which fits your needs.

My suggestion is to select a hotel in the downtown area. This will eliminate precious travel time when sightseeing. Many tour busses routinely stop at the door of the larger hotels. Virtually all these hotels have family rates or discounts of one kind or another.

Three hotels which I can recommend are the Washington Hilton and Towers (providing you are a member of Hilton HHonors for seniors); the Omni Shoreham and the Sheraton Washington. They all offer swimming, tennis (often with instruction if desired), saunas and fine restaurants. If notified in advance, the Hilton will have special gifts for you and your grandchild upon arrival. They also have a toy lending desk, much like a lending library, so your youngster can check out toys or games to keep overnight.

Both the Shoreham and the Sheraton are near Rock Creek Park with its bicycle and jogging trails, bridal path, tennis courts and the National Zoological Park.

These are only three of the many excellent hotels which offer promotional plans. Check with your favorite chain to see what they offer. It pays to shop around.

As far as I am concerned, there is no better way to see Washington than to take the Old Town Trolley. It is a replica of a Victorian-era streetcar with a 90 minute narrated tour of the major attractions. It may be boarded at many of the major downtown hotels. Tickets valid for one day cost $16.00 for adults and $8.00 for children 5 - 12 yrs. There are 17 designated stops including the Mall, Smithsonian Institution, White House, Embassy Row, Georgetown, and Arlington National Cemetery. A trolley passes each stop every 30 minutes and you may get on and off as often as you wish.

On your first touring day, I suggest you inquire at the hotel desk about when the first Trolley pick-up is. Then board and ride around the complete circle listening to the narration and deciding what you want to see first, second etc. According to the age and interests of your grandchild, you may want to eliminate certain places and zero in on others.

Some musts for all ages, in my opinion, are the Capitol, the White House, Lincoln and Jefferson Memorials, at least two of the thirteen museums of the Smithsonian Institution, Arlington National Cemetery, Mt. Vernon, the National Zoo and the Washington Monument.

Although you'll have a wonderful time, you certainly can't see everything in one, two or even three days. Plan on a week if at all possible. Your visit needs to include fun things as well as sightseeing. For example, grab a hot dog and soda from one of the sidewalk vendors after a morning of seeing monuments and institutions and go paddle boating around the Tidal Basin.

If you didn't notify your Congressmen of your planned trip and did not receive special access passes, you may want to consider a Gray Line Tour of the interior of the public buildings. There are two 4-hour tours available, one in the morning and one in the afternoon. The morning tour includes stops at the White House, the Jefferson Memorial, Ford's Theatre and the National Museum of American History. Tickets for the public rooms are included. Keep in mind that the White House is closed to the public on Sundays, Mondays and other days when there are special state events. If this is a high priority to you or your grandchild, you may want to check before you go. Gray Line phone number is (802) 289-1995.

The afternoon tour begins with a walking tour of the U.S. Capitol. Hopefully, you received visitors' gallery passes from your Senators and Representatives. If Congress is in session, do stop and watch, it is most interesting. The galleries are open 9 - 4:30 or when they adjourn. This tour also goes to the Supreme Court Building and the National Air and Space Museum. You may purchase separate tickets for the two tours. If you have your gallery passes, you may want to bypass the afternoon tour and do the other buildings on your own.

On the day you go to Mt. Vernon, you may want to take a boat trip down the Potomac River. The Spirit of Mt. Vernon leaves Pier 4, 6th and Water Sts. at 9 a.m. and 2 p.m. Tuesdays through Sundays and on occasional Mondays most of the year. This five hour narrated cruise allows a two hour stopover at George Washington's estate. Food is available on board. Reservations are recommended. Check the prices which change frequently. Phone (202) 554-8000.

When you leave the Trolley at Arlington National Cemetery, you may, of course, walk to any of the spots of interest in the cemetery. I suggest, however, that you purchase the inexpensive Tourmobile tickets which shuttles you up to the Kennedy gravesites, the Tomb of the Unknowns and Arlington House. On the Tourmobile, as on the Trolley, you can get off the bus and reboard another at your leisure. Don't miss the hourly changing of the Guard at the Tomb of the Unknowns and the eternal flame at President Kennedy's grave.

I feel sure if you and your grandchild spent your entire vacation at the Smithsonian Institution, you would have a wonderful time and come away wishing you could have stayed longer. It is hard to believe that this great institution was founded by a man who was not an American and never even visited America. Yet James Smithson, a British scientist, willed his entire fortune of $500,000.00 to "found in Washington, under the name of the Smithsonian Institution an Establishment for the increase and diffusion of knowledge". Perhaps you should start or conclude your tour of the Smithsonian at the Castle which houses his tomb just to say thanks.

Also housed in the Castle is the administration of the museum, the Information Center, a turn-of-the-century children's room and two theatres which show orientation films. Most of the museums are open 10 a.m. - 5:30 p.m. For information about the day's events, you can call (202) 357-2020.

The following three museums seem to be favorites of most children and are located on the Mall in easy walking distance of each other.

The National Air and Space Museum is at the top of my grandchildren's list. You may touch a moon rock and envision yourself in space. There are breath-taking IMAX films shown in a 5 story theatre. Charles Lindberg's Spirit of St. Louis and the Wright brothers' Flyer are here. There is a planetarium where you can learn about anything imaginable concerning air and space. Free guided tours are offered daily at 10:15 a.m. and 1:00 p.m.

The Museum of Natural History is for lovers of pre-historic culture, dinosaurs and cavemen. A lifesize model of a triceratops guards the entrance and a huge African bull elephant graces the rotunda. A Children's Discovery Room is for hands-on-learning. The fabulous Hope diamond is featured in an extraordinary collection. Guided tours are available daily at 10:30 a.m. and 1:30 p.m. There are also self-guiding audio tours.

The Museum of American History began as the National Cabinet of Curiosities and has grown to contain items from nearly every facet of life. It was here, on the second floor, that Stephanie found the ruby-red slippers from the *Wizard of Oz* she talked about so incessantly I was convinced, for a while, that she'd seen nothing else..

In the Arts and Industries Building you will find the Discovery Theatre which offers a variety of children's plays during the warm months. Call (202) 357-1500 for a schedule.

The best places in Washington for your youngster to shop for souvenirs are in the museum gift shops. Most have a wide array of interesting items at as reasonable a price as you can find. You might want to pass this on to your grandchild for whatever he thinks it is worth.

Good, quick and inexpensive places for lunch when you're sightseeing are the various cafeterias and eateries in most museums and government buildings.

Part of the Smithsonian Institution, but located in Rock Creek Park, is the National Zoological Park. The grounds are open from 8 a.m. and the buildings at 9 a.m. until 5:30 p.m. The indoor and outdoor exhibits house close to 5,000 animals. Upon entering, check the hours for feeding time. Watching the animals being fed is always interesting, for child and adult alike.

The Bureau of Engraving and Printing, which prints money and stamps, is located just south of the Washington Monument grounds. It's interesting and free.

Near Union Station (a Trolley stop) is the Capitol Children's Museum. Here your youngster can touch and play with the exhibits, a learning experience that's fun. There are activities in the arts, theatre, science, humanities and math. The children make crafts to take with them. There is a small admission charge.

Another hands-on program, this time pertaining to the exploration of the sea, storms and early man, is presented in Explorers Hall, National Geographic Society, 17th and M Sts. N.W. This program is free.

Young artists or art lovers won't want to miss the National Gallery of Art at 4th and Constitution Ave. N.W. or the National Museum of American Art (another branch of the Smithsonian Institution) located in the old Patent Office Building between 7th and 9th, G and F Sts. N.W. The National Portrait Gallery is in the building's South wing.

For an excellent example of Gothic architecture, visit the Washington National Cathedral which took 83 years to construct. One of the stained glass windows contains a moon rock. Be sure to note the "Creation" window at the West entrance. It is pale blue in the morning but by late afternoon, as the sun moves across the sky and catches the red in the many glass prisms, its hue is completely changed.

Check a Washington newspaper for spectator sports or theatre events while you are there. There are often productions appropriate for children at Ford's Theatre and the Kennedy Center. If you go to Ford's Theatre, detour across the street to the Petersen House where Lincoln was taken after he was shot and where he died.

I purposely left mentioning the Washington Monument until now because I hope you will make this your very last visit before leaving the city. It is a memorable and fitting climax for your visit. If you are leaving on a Saturday or Sunday, you might want to drive there on your way out of town. You will be able to find adequate parking on these days. The monument is open daily, 8 a.m. until midnight, April Ist until Labor Day and 9 a.m. - 5 p.m. the rest of the year. The earlier you arrive in the morning, the shorter the line will be to enter. Expect a wait though but, believe me, it is worth it, especially to see your youngster's reaction. My granddaughter was entranced when she looked out the first window of the observation room, some 500 feet above the city.

"Oh, look, Grandma," she called excitedly, "there's the White House and the Capitol." Running from one window to another she became more and more excited as she found the Castle of the Smithsonian and the Lincoln Memorial and the Mall and the Reflection Pool and on and on. We spent more than an hour going back and forth looking, remembering, saying goodbye.

It was a wonderful end to a visit to our capital city.

CHAPTER

8

FLORIDA

(Appropriate for boys and girls ages 6 and up)

With grandchildren in tow, my favorite part of Florida is the northeastern coast from St. Augustine to Cocoa Beach. I have found this especially true when traveling with younger children. Sun, sand, surf, space and history abound along this stretch of the Sunshine State.

If you are flying down, the Jacksonville International Airport serves the region. If you are coming by car, you will probably enter on either I-95, which runs north-south, or I-10 which comes from the west. Amtrak also schedules stops in Jacksonville.

Train rides can be true adventures for kids of all ages. Regardless of how you arrive, you will need a car for the rest of your trip. Get directions to Jacksonville Beach, pick up hwy. AlA at the beach and proceed down the coast for about an hour to the oldest city in the United States.

ST. AUGUSTINE.

What child isn't fascinated with the "oldest" this and the "first" that? This city contains it all—the oldest house, the oldest store, the oldest wooden schoolhouse. There is a fountain which legend tells us is the Fountain of Youth. One drink of the spring water and you'll never grow old. Overlooking the water is a massive old Spanish fortress with a moat and turrets and 16 ft. wall for children to run about and explore on their own.

In addition to all this, just south of the city walls, on Anastasia Island are miles of wide, beautiful sand beaches on the Atlantic Ocean.

When you arrive in St. Augustine, you may want to head straight to the Visitor Information Center at 10 Castillo Dr. and pick up a supply of brochures, maps and information about the area before checking into your hotel. This way you can leisurely plan how and what to see first, second, etc.

A decision you will need to make before your trip is where to stay. Do you want to be on the beach? Do you prefer the historical area within walking distance of many historical sites or inland where recreation is the strong point?

The La Fiesta Oceanside Inn is my choice for lodgings on the beach. It is a Spanish style motel with a dune walkover to the beach, a children's playground, swimming pool and, handily, a coin laundry.

Virtually next door to the old fortress is convenient Monterey Inn. Nearby are tennis courts, an ice cream parlor and many historic attractions. The horse drawn carriages and sight-seeing trains stop across the street. There is on premise parking here which is important because parking in St. Augustine is at a premium. Note to remember: when you see a yellow painted curb it means NO PARKING and it is strictly enforced.

If you have a budding golfer, beginning tennis player or serious swimmer, you may opt for the Sheraton Palm Coast, about 1 mile inland, which boasts access to four championship golf courses, 16 tennis courts, a heated pool, exercise equipment and an island playground with waterfalls and ponds.

You might plan a night or so at a hotel in each area.

A walking tour, starting at the old city gates and extending south on narrow St. George St. to the oldest Store Museum then back through the Plaza de la Constitucion, is the best way to see the restoration of old St. Augustine. You can park your car at the visitor's center because none are allowed on St. George St.

Allow at least three hours for a leisurely walk, photography stops and/or visits to points of interest along the way. Pause for a moment at the Spanish Bakery to sample the freshly baked meat turnovers, cookies and bread made from Colonial recipes.

If you and your small charge prefer riding to walking, you can take one or more of seven different open air trolley tours offered by the St. Augustine historical Tours. Non-walkers also might choose the sightseeing trains which provide stop offs at major points of interest and, of course, it's fun to tour around in the colorful horse and carriage rides.

One of the joys of childhood is exploring and, for kids, nothing is more fun than running and poking about in a three century old fort. Park rangers at the Castillo de San Marcos National Museum provide an introductory talk and then you are on you own to peer into the garrison rooms, climb the stairway to the gun deck where cannons are fired Saturdays and Sundays from June through Labor Day.

Regardless of your age, you won't want to miss drinking from Ponce de Leon's Fountain of Youth. On the same grounds are the remains of a Timucuan Indian burial site.

At the historic Old Jail, costumed guides portray the early sheriff and his wife who take you through their living quarters and the prisoners' cells. If you'd like you can sit in a replica of an electric chair.

For youngsters who have never seen an alligator (and want to), try the St. Augustine Alligator Farm southeast on hwy.

AlA. A walkway takes you over and through a rookery and alligator swamp. Wildlife shows are presented hourly.

A two hour musical drama by Paul Green re-enacts the founding of St. Augustine in 1565. It is presented Monday through Saturday at 8:30 p.m., mid-June to late August in the Cross and Sword Amphitheater located about two miles south on AlA. It is enjoyable and informative even for the younger set.

Only 18 miles south of St. Augustine on hwy. AlA, is Marineland of Florida, one of the first exhibits of its kind in the U.S. and still quite good. There are six aquatic shows daily. The dolphin performances and fish feeding exhibits are especially interesting to the younger children. Don't leave after the first 50 minute presentation though. Walk about the grounds and see the penguins and other unusual forms of sea life. There is a movie entitled "Sea Dream" which appeals to children and adults alike. You can easily spend most of a day here and, if you choose to spend the night, you will find a Holiday Inn on the grounds which, in addition to the beach, has two pools, 2 tennis courts, a playground and a restaurant.

DAYTONA BEACH

Heading south once more on AlA you will soon come to Daytona Beach, famous for its 23 mile long, 500 ft. wide (at low tide) expanse of hard packed white sand. It once was an automobile speedway. Cars are now allowed to drive along the packed sand at the waters edge in the daytime. In my opinion, this is not conducive to safe beach play for the children who love to run in and out of the water, fly kites and build sand castles without having to be constantly on the watch for cars.

Despite this, I gave my grandchildren the experience of riding on the vast beach by paying the $5.00 toll and driving the car along the waters edge before saying farewell to Daytona Beach and continuing south toward the Space Coast.

Some miles south, you should turn east on 528 Causeway. This will bring you to Merritt Island, home of the Kennedy Space center, Cape Canaveral Air Force Station, Spaceport USA, U.S. Space Camp Florida and Cocoa Beach. Hopefully, you will have made reservations for lodging at the latter.

Cocoa Beach has numerous good beach-front motels but it is a very popular place, especially if you are fortunate enough to be there at launch time. You may want to call NASA's shuttle hotline (407) 867-4636 to determine any information as to current launches.

Six year-old William and I were able to witness a blast-off from the balcony of our room at the Holiday Inn in Cocoa Beach. It certainly was an experience we won't forget. If you do not have a view of the launch site from your motel, a good spot for viewing is the Cocoa Beach Pier. The pier also has a very good restaurant open daily for dinner and on Sunday for brunch as well. It is fun to eat looking out over the water.

To avoid crowds and assure yourself admission to the theater and bus trip, you need to be at the Spaceport USA before the Center's opening at 9 a.m. to buy your tickets. Allow a minimum of five hours to see the exhibits and theater presentation at the Spaceport and to take the 2 hour bus tour of the Kennedy Center and Cape Canaveral Air Force Station. If your grandchild is an astronaut wanna-be, as mine is, you might spend more than a day here.

The Spaceport contains two IMAX theaters with different presentations and the Kennedy Center sponsors two bus tours. Nothing would satisfy my young aspiring astronaut but to return the second day and see everything including the Air Force Space Museum, the Astronauts Memorial Space Mirror and, of course, the U.S. Space Camp which he hopes to attend in a few years. This camp is great because it encourages the study of math and science in a fun, hands-on scientific manner. We were able to watch the campers in the 4th to 7th grades undergo simulated space training and we too were allowed to experience a space flight aboard a full size shuttle simulator. I came away feeling that I had been born too soon.

SILVER SPRINGS

Rather than retrace the AlA route north to Jacksonville, I suggest you take I95 north to the exit of hwy. 50 west which runs into the Florida Turnpike. Turn north on the Turnpike to Wildwood where you will pick up I75 north to Ocala, home of Florida's Silver Springs. This is about a three hour drive.

There are several motels here so finding good lodging even without advance notice shouldn't be a problem. I do suggest that you allot one full day to see Silver Springs. If you have the afternoon of your arrival free, you might check out Blue Springs State Park about four miles south on U.S. hwy 17. This is reputed to be a great place to spot the endangered manatees. Or, if you are brave enough, there is Wild Waters, a water theme park with a giant wave pool and seven water flume rides.

Silver Springs, estimated to be some 100,000 years old, was once a watering place for prehistoric animals. Fossilized remains of mastodons have been found in and around these artesian springs. This is of interest to most youngsters in this day when even kindergartners can identify dinosaurs by name.

There is an all-inclusive admission so plan to do it all—the Glass-Bottom boat, the Jungle Cruise, the Jeep Safari, the Lost River Voyage and the Doolittle Petting Zoo. The hours are 9 a.m. to 5:30p.m. with extended hours in the summer.

Leaving Ocala and the Silver Springs area, you can choose your route back to Jacksonville. Hwy 40 goes over to Daytona Beach where you can pick up I95 north, or, if you want some more beach time, go over to AlA and retrace your earlier route. Hwy 301 goes straight north passing near Gainesville, home of Florida State University and through Florida's range country. Turn east when you come to I-10 into Jacksonville where you can say a fond farewell to Florida.

CHAPTER

9

GREAT SMOKY MOUNTAIN NATIONAL PARK

(Appropriate for boys and girls ages 5 and up)

Two-thirds of the population of the entire United States lives within a day's drive of the Great Smoky Mountain National Park located on the border between Tennessee and North Carolina. This makes it the most popular tourist attraction and the most visited of all the parks.

It is especially fun for younger children. I usually start taking mine when they are four or five years old. There are misty mountain trails to be explored, shallow, rocky rivers to be waded, ski lifts to carry you to the top of bluish mountain peaks, preserved pioneer villages to visit and a glitzy town with multitudinous hotels and motels, excellent restaurants, candy factories and souvenir shops.

Gatlinburg, Tennessee is where my grandchildren and I choose to stay. Nestled at the foot of Mt. LeConte, stretching for about two miles on the banks of the little Pigeon River, this glittery small town is fascinating to children. While the high degree of commercialization is a turn-off to some, my grandchildren and I love it. The narrow main street (US hwy. 441) is thickly lined on both sides with hotels, motels, restaurants, shops and amusement-park type attractions. It is a town where even the younger children can feel a certain amount of freedom as they walk up and down the streets, dodging in and out of the shops and spending their vacation money.

I suggest staying in one of the centrally located motels or hotels so that almost everything is within walking distance. You might prefer an accommodation which has both indoor and outdoor swimming pools, so the kids can swim regardless of the weather. Gatlinburg is somewhat more expensive than its neighbors Sevierville and Pigeon Forge, but you can walk everywhere, the restaurants are far better and the atmosphere more resort-like.

On the North Carolina side of the mountains, just outside the park, is an authentic Indian Reservation with an amphitheater showing a long-running drama. Nearby is a town where gems are panned for by tourists.

The first day in Gatlinburg is usually the best time to explore the town. First, by taking one or several of the 19th century replica trolleys which carry passengers around the entire area. Then, having selected and prioritized what you want to do and see, start walking.

A word of warning: Be sure to set spending limits for you and your grandchild. It is very easy to go far over budget here in a short period of time.

Sometime that first day you will probably take the chair lift from the middle of town to the top of Crocker Mountain, have your picture taken, view the picturesque surroundings or opt for the observation tower at the corner of Airport Rd. You undoubtedly will visit one of the candy factories to watch the way the sweet delights are made before sampling and, perhaps buying some. The chocolate fudge is my favorite, but my grandchildren all favor the candied apples. Ambling in and out of the multitude of souvenir shops, stopping to play a game in an arcade or have your fortune told by a machine, may take up most of your day.

The Aerial Tramway takes you from downtown, two and one-half miles to the Ober Gatlinburg complex where there is skiing in the winter, an ice skating rink, an alpine slide, a black bear habitat, a sightseeing chair lift to the 3500 ft summit of Mt. Harrison, and cafes with live entertainment.

Be sure to check at the Gatlinburg Convention Center for any special events which might be going on while you are there.

The Guinness World Reconds Museum is fascinating for the younger generation and you might pick up some trivia there, too.

Restaurants in Gatlinburg, are abundant and, for the most part, good. Of course, you may be conned into eating at

McDonalds, Shoneys or the Dairy Queen but, if you can, negotiate with your grandchild and try some others, too. You might try something like this, breakfast at charming Pancake Pantry, lunch at a place of his choice and dinner at the Burning Bush or Pioneer Inn.

One day I suggest you drive the few miles down to Sevierville and eat at the unique Applewood Farmhouse Restaurant located in a flourishing apple orchard. It is open 8 a.m. until 9 p.m. I think both generations will be pleased. If you can't resist outlet shopping, you will pass several as you drive back through Pigeon Forge toward Gatlinburg.

Take a full day for a trip down Little River Road to the 11 mile Cades Cove loop. Years ago, before the area was taken over by the National Park System, farm families carved homesteads in this wilderness. Some of the old barns, rustic churches, mountain cabins and grist mills , preserved by the park, stand silent, allowing newer generations to take a peek at what life once was in these mountains. Plan to spend time here, running about, exploring, imagining. On Saturdays, from dawn until 10 a.m., the loop is reserved for cyclists. If this is of interest to you, bikes can be rented at the Cades Cove Campground.

On the way to or from Cades Cove, be sure to stop by Sugarlands Visitor Center to pick up leaflets and brochures covering the various nature trails, both for hiking and driving, the wild life and any special activities planned by the park rangers.

On another day, head up US 441 into the park, past Sugarlands and on up the ten mile drive to Newfound Gap on the North Carolina border. The scenery is spectacular. Stop to enjoy it. See the weird shapes of the chimney peaks towering above you. Watch along the road for black bears, remembering, of course, not to feed or get out of the car near them. Pause for a snack at a picnic area alongside the rocky river where you may want to doff your shoes and wade out in the cold, clear mountain stream. Take a short hike on one of the many trails leading to a special vista. You may run through some low hanging clouds as you ascend the mountain. This is always fascinating to youngsters.

When you get to Newfound Gap, stop, get out of the car and gaze out over the bluish haze of these massive mountains, you'll see how they got the name, Smoky. Look for the highway winding on down the North Carolina side—a road you will be taking one day soon when you visit the Cherokee Indian Reservation. See an entrance to the famed Appalachian Trail which wends its way from Georgia to Maine.

A seven mile spur road leads from Newfound Gap to Clingman's Dome, the highest point in the park, and all in Tennessee. Take the one-half mile trail up to the concrete spiral walkway tower from which you can survey the panorama spread around you.

When you are ready to bid farewell to Gatlinburg, retrace your route to Newfound Gap and continue on down the mountain to Cherokee, N.C., home of the descendants of those Cherokee Indians who, in 1838, escaped into the mountains thereby avoiding their forced removal over the infamous Trail of Tears to Oklahoma. *Unto These Hills* is the sad story of this tribe told dramatically in the outdoor Mountainside theater nightly except Sunday. I strongly recommend it. Be prepared, though, for your grandchild to come away wanting to give back your land to the Indians. In order to see this drama, it would be wise to check into one of the several motels along the highway rather than drive back over the mountain to Gatlinburg late at night.

Oconaluftee Indian Village is another must. It is a replica of a Native American village of more than 250 years ago. There is a story teller in the seven-sided house, a, herb garden and a variety of craft demonstrations, all put on by authentic Cherokee Indians. My four year old granddaughter was enthralled by the whole program. Having been told that the Indians in the souvenir shops on the highway were Indians but not true Cherokees, she staunchly refused to pose for a picture with one in a chieftain headdress outside a shop.

At the Museum of the Cherokee Indian, across the street from Oconoluftee, the Cherokees do sell some of their traditional crafts, many of which you will have seen demonstrated in the village.

If you have a young rock collector with you, you may want to continue your trip on south on Hwy 441 to Franklin, N.C. the home of the Cowee Valley ruby mines. There are more than a dozen surface mines in the area. Most of them furnish information, equipment and assistance for those who want to search for gems. For about $5.00, you can purchase a pail of dirt to sift through a strainer hopefully to find ruby, sapphire or other mineral chips and, sometimes, even larger stones. There are gem shops in the area which will polish and mount your gems if you desire. You almost always find something and it is great fun to try. There is an annual Gemboree featuring jewelry and gem exhibits and ruby mining field trips in late July.

Unless you particularly want to retrace your trip over the mountain and are headed toward either Knoxville or Chattanooga, TN, I suggest you consider taking the picturesque state hwy 28 west through the scenic southern Appalachians. There is Nantahala Gorge, "land of the noon-day sun", so named by the Indians because it is so deep and so narrow that the sun reaches the bottom only at noon. Fontana Lake, a little farther along, is great for boating and fishing.

This is a wonderful trip for everyone, but especially for your younger grandchildren. It has all sorts of fun, hands-on activities which are also learning experiences. Whether you live near enough to drive from home or choose to fly into the Knoxville Airport and rent a car, I truly believe you and your grandchild will thoroughly enjoy this memorable mountain experience.

CHAPTER

10

HAWAII

(Appropriate for boys and girls ages 12 and up)

From the moment your plane touches down and you receive your welcoming "aloha" and flowered lei, I predict that you and your grandchild will be hooked on Hawaii. The beauty, the near perfect weather, the mystery and paradoxes of these enchanted islands will keep you entranced for as long as you stay and beckon you back as long as you live.

Getting to Hawaii is easy. Many of the leading airlines offer flights between the mainland and the islands. It is a five hour flight from the west coast. Your travel agent will advise you as to the lowest available fare. Be sure to tell him your age and that of your grandchild, it could make a difference in the amount you pay. Any way you look at it though, this is not an inexpensive trip.

To avoid an excessively long flight if you are traveling from the east, you may want to fly into Los Angeles or San

Francisco a day or so early in order to rest and move about a little.

Don't forget the time changes. You will be traveling back toward yesterday. The Islands operate on Hawaiian Standard Time. If it is 9 a.m. in Hawaii, it will be 11 a.m. Pacific time; 12 noon Mountain time; 1 p.m. central time, and 2 p.m. eastern time. Hawaii does not observe daylight saving time, so the time difference may increase an hour if where you live is on daylight time.

When packing, the name of the game on the Islands is casual. Sandals or hiking boots if you are hiking the trails are all you will need for footwear. The island kids go barefoot as much as possible, even to school. Your favorite summer casual clothes, a light sweater for evenings or exploring the volcanoes, underthings and at least two swim suits are basically all you will need.

When we think of Hawaii we usually think of two to five islands. Contrary to popular opinion, though, our fiftieth state consists of 122 islands stretching over a 1500 mile span in the Pacific Ocean. Many of these islands are merely jagged rocks or tiny sandy shoals rising mysteriously from a great volcanic mountain chain deep in the ocean. It might be great fun to sail along and visit and explore many or all of them, but for all practical purposes, this is unlikely if not impossible.

In this chapter we'll concentrate on the two best known and most popular islands: Oahu and Hawaii. Each has its own distinct personality

OAHU

It is very probable that you will fly into the Honolulu International Airport on the island of Oahu. While third in size, Oahu, meaning "shell-gathering place", is the most densely populated and famous of the islands. It boasts Honolulu, the capital city of the state, world renowned Waikiki Beach and the famous landmark, Diamond Head. Pearl Harbor, which will probably mean nothing to your grandchild, but is probably forever etched in your memory, is here also.

Whether you are renting a car or not, I suggest you stop by one of the car rental counters in the airport and pick up a free *Oahu Drive Guide.* It contains a wealth of tourist information. Certainly having a car at your disposal is the best way to see everything you want at your own pace. Driving in Honolulu is no worse than in any other U.S. city. Rush hours can be frustrating and one way streets confusing, but not impossible. If you want a rental car, be sure to reserve it well in advance of your arrival. On Oahu, as opposed to some of the other islands, it is possible to use other means of transportation and see the island.

The weather in Hawaii is usually fantastic; balmy, sunny with gorgeous blue skies. The pace of the natives is slow so it's easy to make this a restful, relaxing vacation. Flexibility in planning your days here is the key word. Don't push. Don't rush. Do what you want at as leisurely a pace as you and your grandchild desire. If you want to spend the day at the beach or around the pool, do it. If you want to browse through the shops, hike in the mountains or take a sightseeing tour, do that.

The Bus is a man-made wonder on the island which circulates all through Honolulu, into central Oahu and along the north coastline. I believe the best buy in Hawaii is the four hour, 80 mile trip around the island's Koolan Mountains, including much of the Windward Coast for 85 cents (correct change only, please). If you have the time, I suggest you take this trip on your first day to orient yourselves to the island and then decide what to do, when and how. Be sure to buy the nominally priced *The Bus Guide* and/or *Honolulu and Oahu by the Bus.* Both are extremely helpful when planning.

Taxis are very expensive. A cab from the airport to downtown costs approximately $25.00. Many of the hotels run their own shuttles at a fraction of that cost.

There are boat, bus, van, helicopter and even submarine tours ready and waiting for you. Study the brochures in your hotel lobby and don't hesitate to ask questions if there is something you don't understand. There's a day tour, which is likely to appeal to your youngster, led by native Islanders that includes an island tour by van, then some Boogie boarding (surfing on a small board) and snorkeling (accompanied by certified life guards) from Waimanalo beach. Call True Value Tickets and Tours 923-5911 for information and reservations.

Surfing is synonymous with Hawaii, especially for the young. I don't know of any teen or even pre-teen who doesn't want to try it. It is a dangerous sport, though, and even the pros study the swells, the seasons and act accordingly. If your grandchild is as determined to try it as mine was, try the Haleiwa Surf Center at 66167 Haleiwa Rd. where surfing is taught free of charge on week-ends between April and October when the surf is low. Waikiki Beach is certainly one of the most famous of all the surfing spots in the world and my grandson was eager to try it there. The lessons were very expensive and we were advised that its waves should be avoided by all but the experts. I had to say no.

For swimming (and you wouldn't want to come to the islands without doing that) stick to beaches where there are lifeguards. But beware, sometimes there are hazardous currents under the gentlest-seeming waves. Two beaches that are great for swimming, sunbathing, flying kites, and generally having fun are Ala Moana Park and Goat Island off North Shore's Kalanai Point. Sans Souci, across from Kapiolani Park also has shallow water safe for children.

If you want an Oceanside hotel or condominium on Waikiki (and who doesn't?) expect to pay for it. Prices range from $160.00 up for a double room. There are many in the more moderate range only a block or so from the beach and a few in the inexpensive range. Prices are somewhat less near Diamond Head. Travel agents are invaluable in helping you find what will be adequate for your needs. They may refer you to a bed and breakfast or a group tour if individual plans are beyond your financial reach. Be honest about your price range and other considerations.

Regardless of where you stay, you will want to visit at least one of the larger hotels. At the Royal Hawaiian, often called the "Pink Lady" because of its somewhat garish pink color, you will want to stroll through the wonderful palm gardens down to the prime beachfront. Try to go on Monday for the traditional Royal Luau at its Coconut Grove. It is by far the best of the luaus and something which must be experienced at least once.

Just down the ocean walk is the Halekulani Hotel built on the site of a 1917 hotel what was the setting for the first of the Charlie Chan detective stories, *The House Without a Key.* You and your young mystery-book lover may want to read this on the plane going over. If you enjoyed *Kidnapped* or *A Child's Garden of Verses,* you will want to visit the fine old Sans Souci and sit and meditate as Robert Louis Stevenson did under a hau tree.

If your grandchild is a teenager, she or he will probably want to learn the hula. At 10:00 a.m. on Tuesdays, Wednesdays, and Thursdays the Royal Hawaiian Glee Club puts on a one hour show ending in a mass class in hula instruction. It is called the Kodak Hula Show and is in Kapislani Park. It is usually crowded, so get there early. The doors open at 8:30 a.m.

Also in Kapiolani Park are the Honolulu Zoo and the Waikiki Aquarium, both open daily.

The Hawaiian Childrens' Museum has an excellent hands-on science center which kids love. This is located at Dole

Cannery Square. There is a shuttle from the cannery to Waikiki daily. Call 522-0040 for times.

You may have to wait in line and your youngster may argue about going, but don't miss Pearl Harbor and the Arizona Memorial. If your grandchild doesn't know about the morning of Dec. 7, 1941, tell him. If your memory is vague, read up on it or take a sightseeing tour to it. It is Hawaii's most popular tourist attraction and rightly so. It is open daily, 7:30 a.m. to 5:00 p.m. The last program begins at 3:00 p.m.

Next door is the USS Bowfin / Pacific Submarine Museum. It is interesting to anyone who love submarines. The Punchbowl, where more than 35,000 American servicemen and women are buried, is very busy on Sundays when visitors come to honor the dead by laying leis and bouquets of flowers on the graves. World War II buffs will want to visit the U.S. Museum of Hawaii on Kalia and Saratoga Rds. Open Tues. through Sun. 10 a.m. - 4:30 p.m.

Of course you will have seen the massive Diamond Head looming protectively over the island since you arrived but, to get to it, you need to take the road off Monsarat Ave. near 18th Ave. which leads through a tunnel onto the floor of the crater. If you are physically up to a hike, take the .7 mile dirt trail through another tunnel and up a steep 99 step stairway to a gun emplacement. Beyond, three spiral staircases and a steel ladder lead to the crater rim and the most spectacular view of wonderful Waikiki.

HAWAII

The big Island of Hawaii, as its name implies, is the largest in the chain of islands. Because of the fountains of lava erupting from its two active volcanoes, it is always increasing in size.

You will fly in to either General Lyman Field or Keahole Airport. If you want to visit the black beaches on the Kahala or Kona coasts, you will arrive at the latter. The former provides access to Hilo and the Hawaii Volcanoes National Park.

If you are on the island for only one day, I suggest you take a Gray Line Tour to the National Park. The guides are well versed in geology and the vehicles will pick you up at the airport or your hotel. Phone 329-9337.

The more adventurous of you may want to rent a car and drive about and perhaps do some hiking. Keep in mind that the roads are so often subject to interruption, such as an earthquake, pumice drift or lava flow, that you may find the road suddenly closed. Road crews are always at work renewing them, but it can be uncertain. If you choose to drive, take hwy. 11 from the airport to Hilo in the park. It is a breathtakingly beautiful and interesting drive. The 11 mile Crater Rim Drive around the Kilauea Caldera is too. Legend has it that Pele, goddess of volcanoes, makes her home at the rim of Halemalumalu Crater within the Kitauea Caldera. You will see bouquets of flowers, leis, fruit, food and drink left on the rim as offerings to Pele, who remains a very popular and respected pagan goddess.

Seeing the lava flows and tubes, the volcanic ash, the pahochoes, the pumice drift - often with curtains of fire and rivers of hot lava - is certainly reason enough to visit this ever changing island. Be sure to stop at Thurston Lana Tube and walk through this old volcanic cave.

If you have a second day in the park, drive down the Chain of Craters Road where lava is usually flowing to the sea. Trails both long and short abound and are wonderful, out-of-this-world experiences. Always stay on marked roads and trails and obey signs regarding closings and detours. For current updates of volcanic activity, keep your car radio tuned to AM 530.

Volcanic Village, just outside the park, has a lodge, cottages and bed and breakfasts.

Another popular way to see the island is to take an aerial tour. There are several departing from Lyman Field in Hilo.

Regardless of the number of islands you visit, whether it is one or more you surely will fall in love with our 50th state. The beauty, the relaxed atmosphere and the friendliness of the Islanders make it an ideal inter-generational vacation.

CHAPTER

11

NEW YORK CITY

(Appropriate for boys and girls ages 12 and up)

Certainly the largest city in the United States, New York City, to me, is also the most exciting. It is a smorgasbord of culture, history, sports, recreation and fun. No matter where your grandchild's primary interests lie, the Big Apple can satisfy his or her appetite.

Extensive advance planning is essential, however. The two of you need to sit down together, study your tourist materials, set priorities and make advance decisions as to what you want to see and do.

Check the Sunday edition of the New York Times (most public libraries have them) to see what special events, sports activities, plays, concerts etc. are planned for the time you plan to be there.

I definitely do not recommend driving in New York City unless you have done it before and are comfortable with the traffic. Even then, don't go in during rush hours (7-9:30 a.m. and 4:30-6:30 p.m.). Keep in mind that most avenues are one way, north or south, while numbered streets are all one way (even numbered street *usually* eastbound and odd numbers westbound).

Very likely you will fly into one of the three airports which serve the city, LaGuardia, Kennedy or Newark, N.J. Taxis from the airports to midtown Manhattan are quite expensive and I suggest you take one of the express busses from the airport to the Port Authority Bus Terminal at W. 42nd St. and 8th Ave. From there you can take a taxi to your hotel at a far more reasonable price.

There are an abundance of good hotels in Mid-Manhattan. While expensive, they are so well located (many within walking distance of theaters, museums, restaurants etc.) that it will be worth the cost. Remember, when you call for reservations, ask for any discounts which might be available to you. When deciding on a hotel, take into consideration the special events you will want to see. For example, if you have a young drama lover with you, be aware that most Broadway theaters are located just east or west of Broadway between 40th and 52nd Sts.

Music lovers and dance enthusiasts will undoubtedly want to attend events at Lincoln Center, located 62nd to 66 Sts. between Columbus and Amsterdam Aves.

Budding young artists will want to start their museum trek with the huge and wonderful Metropolitan Museum of Art at 5th Ave. at 82nd Street.

Sports fans may choose to be near Madison Square,Garden where the Knicks play basketball and the Rangers play hockey. This is located between 7th and 8th Aves. and 31st and 33rd Streets.

When you first arrive in the city and have checked into your hotel, go outside and walk down the canyon-like streets, looking up at the massive skyscrapers. It is an experience like no other, especially if it is your first trip to New York City. On subsequent trips, these vertical monsters will seem to shrink in height somewhat.

As usual, a sightseeing bus tour should be on the agenda for your first full day in any city and New York is certainly no exception. There are innumerable tours ranging from about two hours to all day. You may want to select an all day tour or shorter ones which encompass much that you want to see. There are special bus tours now which take you all around the city, stopping at various locations, i.e. Greenwich Village (a must for teens) and museum mile. You pay one fee and can hop on and off the bus at designated locations as often as you wish. Ask at your hotel desk for information about the various bus tours available.

As a whole, children and grown-ups love New York City. It is different, exciting. There is so much to see, to do, to savor, experience and enjoy, you can't do it all in a week or a month or even a year, but you can have an unforgettable experience. I'm now going to mention some things or places to see which my grandchildren and I have particularly enjoyed and/or may not have been covered in your sightseeing tour.

By all means, take the elevator to the 86th floor of the Empire State Building and go out on the walkway for a fantastic view of the city. Although this building is not as tall as the World Trade Center (you may want to go there, too), the view is far better.

The Statue of Liberty is also a must. If your city tour did not include a boat trip out to this giant, you can take the ferry from Battery Park in Lower Manhattan daily from 9:30 to 3:30. Return trips are every 90 minutes. If your family came to this country through nearby Ellis Island, you can combine a visit there with your trip to the Statue of Liberty. You'll enjoy sharing the experience of entering this vast, rather intimidating building (now restored for the public's enjoyment with exhibits, gift shop, etc.) just as your ancestors did, with your grandchild—especially those over 10 years old. The names of many immigrants are engraved on plaques outside the building.

Speaking of ferry rides, a trip on the Staten Island Ferry gives you a wonderful view of lower Manhattan and the round trip fare is free. Where else can you find such a bargain? Do avoid the commuter rush hours, though.

Radio City Music Hall is something to be remembered forever. The chandeliers here are the world's largest; the theatre is enormous and the stairway looks as if it came directly from a royal palace in Europe. Guided tours from the lobby are hourly from 10-5p.m. Monday through Friday and 11-5 on Sundays. The stage shows, featuring the world-famous Rockettes, are always a treat for youngsters, especially if you have a granddaughter. You might find her kicking her heels high after seeing this show.

Adjacent to Rockefeller Center in the G.E. building are the NBC television studios. Daily one hour tours leave the foyer from 9:30 a.m. to 4:30 p.m. if you are up early you may want to join the group of eager fans outside during the morning TODAY show. It's traditional for the hosts of the show to come out and talk to the street audience periodically throughout the two hour show.

If shopping is on your agenda, don't overlook Macy's, reputed to be the world's largest department store or Bloomingdale's, Manhattan's most famous.

The Bronx Zoo, the largest urban zoo in the United States, boasts a Wild Asia exhibit through which elephants, tigers and other such animals roam relatively free through a forty acre wilderness. They can be viewed from a monorail.

If your grandchild has studied Edgar Allen Poe, he may want to visit Poe cottage where Poe lived for the last three years of his unhappy life. It was here that his wife died and he wrote "Annabel Lee", his touching tribute to her.

The American Museum of Natural History is a joy for all ages. The largest blue sapphire ever found is on display in the Hall of Meteorites. The Hayden Planetarium has special children's shows on Saturday mornings.

Want to try some ice skating? The Rockefeller Plaza Rink and the Wollman Memorial Rink in Central Park are open in the winter. The New York City Rink in Flushing Meadows is open all year round.

The huge, pastoral patch of green in the middle of a sea of steel and brownstone is famous Central Park. It is here that Shakespeare reigns supreme - and free - in the summer outdoor theater. You can also attend a free performance of the New York Philharmonic here in the summer. There is a lake with boat rentals, bicycle trails, restaurants and jogging paths. But be warned: Central Park is fine to visit in the daylight hours, but should be visited at night only in large groups and for special events.

Theater tickets, which are expensive, are available for many shows at a discount if you are willing to wait until the day of the performance and stand on line at the TKTS booth in Times Square or the one in the lobby of 2 World Center. For evening performances, the booths are open Mon. through Sat. from 3-8:00 p.m. and at 10 a.m. to 2:00 p.m. for Wed. and Sat. matinees. Only cash or travelers cheques are accepted.

Half-price tickets for a random offering of current shows are available from the Music and Dance Booth in Bryant Park, 5th Ave. and 42nd St. Tues. through Sunday noon to 3:00pm. and 4:00 to 7p.m.

Tickets to the major television shows can be obtained through the guest relations office of the networks. There may be a minimum age requirement so be sure to ask when calling. For NBC, call (212) 664-3058; for CBS, (212) 975-2476 and for ABC, (212) 456-3537.

If you and your grandchild enjoy walking, you might want to try some of the various guided walking tours sponsored by the Municipal Art Society., (212) 935-3950; the Museum of the City of New York (212) 534-1672; City Walkers (212) 989-2456, or the Big Onion Walking Tour (212) 439-1090.

Whether it is the flickering lights of the soaring mid-town skyscrapers; the hustle and bustle of rush hour; the ethnic neighborhoods like Chinatown and Little Italy or the established arts—music, dance, theater—you surely will be entranced by this sensational city.

It was a visit my grandson, Philip, and I will forever treasure and so, I believe, will you.

CHAPTER

12

THE SOUTHWEST

(Appropriate for children ages 10 and up)

If you live in the East, you are in for a treat just seeing the varied topography of this area. It is so unique and beautiful with its deserts, mountains, canyons and forests.

The more interesting spots for inter-generational exploring lie in the northern section of Arizona, in the vicinity of Flagstaff. Regretfully, major airlines do not service either the regional Flagstaff airport or the one in Tusayan just outside the Grand Canyon Village. But Amtrak trains stop regularly in the middle of Flagstaff as do Greyhound busses. So, unless you are driving or coming by train or bus, I suggest you fly into Arizona's capital city of Phoenix, rent a car and drive north some 200 miles to the Grand Canyon.

Although there are Gray Line tours and scenic flights to several of the nearby points of interest, having a car at your disposal will be an enormous convenience and give you a great deal more flexibility. This is important when traveling with the younger generation.

Leaving Phoenix, take I-17 north. After about 90 miles, plan to stop at Montezuma Castle National Monument. It contains ruins of an ancient cliff dwelling built in the 12th or 13th century. The five story castle is believed to have been inhabited by the Sinqgua Indians. Other ruins dot the nearby cliffs. A self-guiding trail has excellent views of the area. My granddaughter was fascinated and we spent more time there than we had planned. There is a picnic area if you are prepared with a take-along lunch. We were not, but wished we had been as there weren't many roadside eateries available.

Seeing the Grand Canyon is undoubtedly your primary reason for this trip, but there are other places of interest in the area which should be considered if you have the time.

When you have found a motel in Flagstaff, before or after you visit the Grand Canyon, take a day trip east on I-40 first to the Meteor Crater and on to the Petrified Forest and Painted Desert.

Meteor Crater is a huge hole blasted by a meteorite 22,000 years ago. Located six miles south of I-40 on a well marked road, it is about 38 miles east of Flagstaff. While you cannot hike into the crater you can see it, hear the audio presentation and read about it. Fascinating.

Going east, about 12 miles past Holbrook, you will come to the Petrified Forest National Park where erosion is unearthing a fossilized prehistoric forest of brilliantly colored, gigantic trees lying prone and broken over the ground. Near the south entrance is the Long Log Walk, from which you can get a good view of these bright stone logs. Numerous fossil bones and plants have been found in the park giving rise to the theory that this area was once roamed by the early dinosaurs.

The park is open 8 a.m. to 5 p.m. daily and scenic 28 mile drive runs through it. Near the northern entrance you can view the Painted Desert, a vast expanse of sand dunes which, at different times of the day, take on a variety of colors.

Rather than retracing your steps, I suggest you enter at the north entrance from I-40 and exit at the south gate which will put you on hwy. 180, 18 miles southeast of Holbrook. Go back to Holbrook and take I-40 west to return to Flagstaff.

Keep in mind that it is illegal to collect plants, rocks, sand or pieces of petrified wood inside the park. Violations incur heavy fines and sometimes prison. The gift shops in the area sell a variety of specimens collected from private areas outside the park. So wait and buy your souvenirs there.

If you are a hiker, another interesting day would be to take hwy. 89 twelve miles north of Flagstaff to the Sunset Crater, one of the many volcanoes (many still active) in the San Francisco Volcanic Field. There are many trails leading into the San Francisco peaks and, even if you aren't a walker, you can take the chair lift from the Fairfield Snowbowl almost to the top of Mt. Agassiz (12,350 ft.) for some spectacular views.

For anyone looking for a more strenuous walk, try the Walnut Canyon National Monument located about 10 miles east of Flagstaff off I-40. It has steep steps leading down to the Visitor Center.

Now for the pièce de résistance—the Grand Canyon of the Colorado, certainly one of our national treasures. Only 84 miles north of Flagstaff via I-40 W to Williams and hwy. 64 north, is the South Rim of the Canyon. Very likely this will be your destination as it is easier to get to than the North Rim and has far more tourist facilities. Also, it is open all year.

The views from the two rims differ considerably. Both are extremely interesting and you might want to visit both. From the Grand Canyon Village at the South Rim, it is 214 miles to the Grand Canyon Lodge on the North Rim. This scenic drive passes through a portion of the Navajo Reservation, the Painted Desert, Kaibab National Forest and over the Navajo Bridge at the northeast end of the park. An engineering masterpiece, this bridge is 616 ft. long and 467 ft. high.

Assuming that you are going to the South Rim as we did, you will find a variety of motels in Tusayan, nine miles south of Grand Canyon Village and even more in the Village just outside the entrance to the park.

If it is at all possible (and you will need to make your reservations well in advance), try to stay in one of the picturesque old hotels on the rim inside the park. My choices are either Bright Angel or El Tovar. They are expensive, but it is well worth the price to be able to walk outside and view the beauty and grandeur of the canyon anytime you choose. For accommodation reservations in the park, write Grand Canyon National Park Lodges, P.O. Box 699, Grand Canyon National Park, AZ 86023 or call (520) 638-2401.

In case you haven't visited the Grand Canyon in some years, you will find changes. Passenger cars are no longer allowed on the West Rim Drive during the summer. Free minibus service is available along this drive from Memorial Day through September. Sightseeing busses, offering a variety of tours, depart from the lodges within the park.

I recommend the Combination Tour which lasts six hours and is priced at $19.00 for adults and half that for children. It is an excellent narrated tour. For schedules and reservations. call Bright Angel Transportation Desk (520)638-2631 ext. 6015 or 6016.

At sunset, regardless of where you stay, you must walk out to Hopi Point and onto the Bright Angel Trail as it winds across the Tonto Plateau to see the shadows magically changing the vistas. The best place to watch the sun rise is Mather Point, some distance east of the visitor center. No matter where you are and what time of day it is, the views are magnificent.

Helicopter and airplane tours of the canyon leave the Grand Canyon Airport in Tusayan throughout the day. Also in Tusayan is the Grand Canyon IMAX Theatre which presents an interesting, informative the film called "Grand Canyon —The Hidden Secrets".

For inter-generational travel, I really do not recommend the one day muleback trips which go down to the canyon floor (although I am sure your grandchild would opt for it in a second). If you are in excellent physical form and very brave, however, I'm sure it would be a memorable trip. You might want to spend the night at the Phantom Ranch if you decide to go. Reservations for this, of course, need to be made well in advance.

A relatively easy walking trail leads along the rim of the canyon between Maricopa Point on the West Rim to the Yauapai Museum. It is recommended for casual hikers and children.

Back down toward Phoenix, you may want to take U.S. 89A south from Flagstaff through Red Rock Country and Oak Creek Canyon. This canyon certainly cannot compare with the Grand Canyon, but its sheer walls are vividly striped with color and, more important, you can drive through it. Slide Rock State Park near there is a natural water chute where you can swim and slide across large large, smooth rocks in the middle of the river. No doubt a great joy to your traveling companion if not to you.

At Sedona you will probably turn east and pick up I-17 southward into Phoenix for your return home.

As our airplane waited its turn to taxi down the runway, I turned to my ten year old granddaughter.

"What did you think?" I asked. "Awesome," was her only comment.

What more could you ask?

CHAPTER

13

YELLOWSTONE AND GRAND TETON NATIONAL PARKS

(Appropriate for boys and girls ages 11 and up)

In all the rugged grandeur of the Rockies, there is no place more interesting—to any age—than Yellowstone National Park and nowhere more fun than Grand Teton National Park. Separated by only sixty miles, a visit to these two very different parks can be done in one vacation.

You probably will fly into Jackson, Wyoming. This airport actually is within the boundaries of Grand Teton Park so when you land, you are there.

While there are shuttle buses which run between the parks and tours within the parks, I strongly suggest you rent a car if at all possible so that you can go and come at your own pace.

Be sure to take your Golden Age Passport (for ages 62 and over) for free admission to both parks. Also, don't forget hiking boots for you and your grandchild. Even those who say they are non-hikers will find themselves doing considerable walking and comfortable boots are a necessity.

I recommend that you plan to circle Yellowstone Park first, then come back and spend the remainder of your time at Grand Teton. Before you leave for this geological wonderland though, I need to warn you to **keep a close watch on your grandchildren while in the park.** There are safe, established boardwalks between and next to the bursts of scalding water and bubbling mud pools in all the thermal areas. Just be certain you and those in your charge stay on these walkways at all times.

Another warning, which you will see posted throughout the park but cannot be emphasized too much, is **Do Not Feed or Touch the Wildlife.** These animals are wild and should be viewed only from a distance. Don't allow any hopping out of the car to take a picture of that cute bear cub. Remember, the mother bear is nearby and does not need media coverage.

The drive from Jackson to Old Faithful Lodge in Yellowstone takes about two and a half hours, so you can judge whether to spend the night in Jackson or go on to Old Faithful that day. You will want to spend at least one night in the gigantic, log-built Old Faithful Inn and Lodge, possibly the most beautiful lodge in America. Reservations must be made far in advance for all the accommodations in both these parks.

Write P.O. Box 165, Yellowstone Park, WY 82190-0165 or call (307) 344-7311.

For more than a hundred years, Old Faithful Geyser has been erupting every 78 minutes (with occasional exceptions). Because of its frequency, this is the most popular geyser in the park. Approximate schedules for its performance are displayed daily in the nearby visitor center. You will want to view this phenomenon several times during your visit.

Two miles of boardwalk lead from Old Faithful to scores of geysers in the area. The Grand Geyser bursts forth on the average of twice a day. For several minutes this giant sends spurts of water some 200 ft. into the air. Check the prediction of eruptions and see it if at all possible. Near the end of the walkway is the deep blue Morning Glory Pool, its color determined by the algae.

Leaving Old Faithful, take the loop road up past the paint pots, large, colorful springs of hot clay. Along the banks of the Firehole River you will probably find buffalo grazing lazily. At the MidwayGeyser Basin is the Grand Prismatic Spring. In the Norris Basin you need to take separate trails, one to see the Steamboat Geyser, the tallest in the world, and the other to see the Echimus Geyser. Take your time on this part of your journey. Make many stops and walk about the designated areas to really take in the wonder. You may be sure your grandchild will be fascinated. She may not be all that excited about the gorgeous mountain scenery around you, but she will be thrilled with the geological marvels.

It will take most of the day for you to arrive at Mammouth Hot Springs near the Montana line and the site of park headquarters. Well-marked trails allow safe viewing of the crusty tier upon tier of colorful, steaming stone cascading down the misty Mountainside.

Here are Mammoth Hot Springs Hotel and Cabins. I cannot recommend the cabins, they are too basic for me. The hotel, although nothing like Old Faithful Inn, is adequate. You may choose to go out of the park to nearby Gardiner, Montana where there are several motels such as the Best Western and Comfort Inns.

Back on the loop road heading east you will come to Mt. Washburn, the park's highest peak. If you are up to an all-day hike, the trek to the lookout tower is a most enjoyable one and the view of the ice packed peaks of the Beartooth Mts. is spectacular. Another shorter, more leisurely trail leads to the spray-drenched base of Tower Falls.

Turning south, the loop road leads alongside the Yellowstone River as it rushes and roars between the steep, mineral stained cliffs and plummets over the narrow waterfall of the Grand Canyon of the Yellowstone. Vistas from both north and south are breathtaking. Viewing from the north side of the canyon, though, may have more appeal to your grandchild because of its proximity to stores and snack bars.

If you suddenly smell something reminiscent of a garbage dump, it is probably the Mud Volcano, certainly the ugliest and most foul-smelling in all the thermal region. For the brave at heart (or those with little or no olfactory sense), you may want to take the mile long boardwalk over smelly mud to the bare shores of Sour Lake.

Only a short distance south, you will come upon the crystalline beauty of Yellowstone Lake, North America's largest Alpine lake. Cruises, rowboats, motor launches and fishing expeditions are for hire, so take your pick and enjoy.

Unless you plan to return to Old Faithful Inn for another night (and I must admit I find that hard not to do), you may want to spend your last night in Yellowstone here on the lake. Yellowstone Hotel is a grand, old-style comfortable hotel. There are cabins also which I cannot recommend.

Leaving Yellowstone and driving the few miles through a dense, green forest, you again enter Grand Teton National Park. Now is the time for you and your grandchild to relax, really get acquainted and have fun with each other in one of the most beautiful spots in the world. Regardless of your interests, you are going to find things you both will enjoy.

My preference for accommodations in the park is the Jackson Hole Lodge in the shadow of the Grand Tetons and overlooking Jackson Lake. The more expensive rooms are, quite naturally, those with a view of the Tetons. I can settle for one of the others because the view from the enormous windows in the lobby or in the Blue Heron Lounge is enough for me and my grandchild, Jan, who didn't come for the view anyway. I most admit, though, that she was impressed when we saw a moose grazing down by the lake.

Other facilities include Colter Bay Village Cabins, Signal Mountain Lodge and small Jenny Lake Lodge. For reservations anywhere in the park, write the Grand Teton Lodge Co., P.O. Box 240, Moran WY 83013 or call (307) 543-2811. Reservations are essential in the summer.

Hiking is a favorite activity in these parts, certainly because of the stunning views at every turn in the trail. An easy and popular walk is along the shore of Leigh Lake under imposing, 12,000 ft. high Mount Moral. Another circles the south shore of Jenny Lake to Hidden Falls. If you are particularly adventurous, you might consider the five mile trek from Lupine Meadows to the tree line. It is strenuous (believe me), but the view of the amphitheater and Surprise lakes are stunning.

The roads around Jackson Hole are flat so that bicycling becomes a wonderful activity. Even if you haven't ridden for years, you'll soon realize it is something you never forget and, of course, you'll have a great mentor in your grandchild. Bikes are for rent in Jackson.

A must is to take a float trip down the Snake River. Whether you opt for the scenic, the exciting white water, the luncheon trip, the evening wildlife or an overnight cruise is up to you. I guarantee you'll have fun.

Horseback riding on horses especially bred for the mountain terrain, is a wonderful way to explore the park. If you are not comfortable on a horse, you may prefer a wagon ride with dinner along the trail.

There are many companies which sponsor the above mentioned activities. Shop around or ask at your hotel desk about availability and price of those which interest you.

This is a different and exciting trip. It is one which can be very bonding—grandchild to grandparent—and will live in memory long after the photographs have faded.

CHAPTER

14

HERE AND THERE

Every section of this great nation of ours has a multitude of opportunities for wonderful inter-generational travel. Some may be so close to your home that you haven't considered them, others may seem to be too far away. Take South Dakota for example.

SOUTH DAKOTA

It isn't served by Amtrak and has only two major airports. Yet, if you fly into Rapid City, you are only 24 miles northeast of Mt. Rushmore National Memorial where the world-famous stone carvings of the faces of George Washington, Abraham Lincoln, Thomas Jefferson and Theodore Roosevelt are etched into the Mountainside. And, only 17 miles farther south, is the still unfinished massive stone carving of Crazy Horse.

Turn northwest from Rapid City for less than fifty miles to Deadwood, reputedly one of the wild west's wildest gold rush towns and burial place of Wild Bill Hickok and Calamity Jane. Farther north is Spearfish, famous for the Black Hills Passion Play which is held three times a week throughout the summer.

Across the state, about sixty miles northwest of Sioux Falls is the town of De Smet, known as "Little Town on the Prairie". You may tour eighteen of the sites Laura Ingalls Wilder mentions in her autobiographical books. Keep in mind, though, the TV location for those stories is in southeast Kansas, near Independence.

CARLSBAD CAVERNS

Still in the west, but far south in the little visited southwest corner of New Mexico, is the Carlsbad Caverns National Park. Too amazing a geological spectacle to miss if at all possible, its nearest city is El Paso, TX.

The Caverns are open daily in summer from 8:30 a.m. to 6:30 p.m. Their last entry is at 3:30 p.m., in time for the nightly exiting of the millions of migratory bats which make their home during the day hanging upside down from the ceiling of the cave. At about dusk, black clouds of these small creatures fly in spirals out of the mouth of the cave and spread out for miles searching for food. It is a phenomena you definitely do not want to miss. Park Rangers are present to answer questions and give you information.

HARRISBURG, PA.

Ten miles east of Pennsylvania's capital city of Harrisburg is a town called Hershey. With streets named Cocoa and Chocolate and streetlights in the shape of Hershey's kisses, it is indeed the chocolate capital of the world.

You can take an automated mini-train ride through Hershey Chocolate World and see, step by step, how chocolate is made. At the end of the tour be sure to stop in the gift shop/cafe and gorge yourselves on an enormous chocolate sundae. Hersheypark, which began in the early nineteen hundreds as a recreational park for the Hershey factory workers, is now a huge amusement park.

WILLIAMSPORT, PA.

About an hour's drive up hwy. 15 is Williamsport, Pa. Your grandchild undoubtedly will know about the town, even if you don't. Famous as host to the Little League World Series each August, it also has the Little League Baseball Museum, a must for any Little Leaguer or ex-Little Leaguer.

NIAGARA FALLS, NY

In the northeast corner of New York State, on the Canadian border, are the Niagara Falls. Highly commercialized on both the American and Canadian sides, you need to keep in mind that you came to see the Falls and avoid many of the tourist traps.

The best view from the American side is the Prospect Point Observation Tower or its base. On the Canadian side it is Queen Victoria Park. I strongly suggest that you view these cataracts from both points. If you are there for only one day, and you don't want to drive across the International Bridge into Canada, you may take either the Bedore U.S. and Canadian Boat and Van Tour or the Boat or Bus Tour. The Bedore Tour leaves from the Howard Johnson at the Falls; the Boat and Bus Tour from the bus station at 343 4th St. Both include the Maid of the Mist boat trip, an absolute must for all ages.

If you plan to spend the night at Niagara, my recommendation is to stay on the Canadian side within easy walking distance of the Falls so you can take in the impressive nightly illumination of this natural wonder.

VIRGINIA

Traveling through the State of Virginia is virtually a non-stop history lesson. Your grandchild will never realize how much she is learning, she'll be having so much fun.

From Richmond, the state capital, to the east lies the historic Tidewater Triangle, made up of Jamestown, Williamsburg and Yorktown where the United States was born. To the northwest and south of this old city, which was once the capital of the confederacy, are the civil war battlefields and memorials-Homes of many famous Americans such as George Washington, Thomas Jefferson, James Monroe and James Madison dot the state.

If you have elementary age grandchildren, a driving trip through this beautiful state with stops in the mountains, at the beach and at the historical spots in which he is interested can be a wonderful experience.

Strung along the North Carolina coast from near the Virginia line to Cape Lookout are a series of barrier islands called the Outer Banks. If you are looking for fine, warm water beaches, you'll find them here.

Kill Devil Hills is where the Wright brothers did their early flying experiments. Kitty Hawk, where the Wright Brothers National Memorial stands, commemorates Orville's first powered flight in 1903. This is a great place to visit and so is Roanoke Island, the site of Sir Walter Raleigh's "Lost Colony". Nothing authentic survived on Roanoke, but three miles north of Manteo, is an Oceanside outdoor amphitheater where an impressive drama. "The Lost Colony" is performed daily except Saturday at 8:30 p.m. This rates a long "Yes" and thumbs up by my grandchildren.

CHAPTER

15

HERITAGE TOURS

Perhaps the best of all inter-generational trips is a heritage tour. This is where you help your grandchildren discover their roots. Seeing the places where parents, grandparents, maybe even great grandparents lived, attended school and worked is of great interest, even to very young children.

Your trip could be as short as around your town if you, your parents, your children and grandchildren were born and still live in the same town. Unless you live in the same house, a trip to where great grandpa was born, even if the house is no longer there, is a good place to start the tour, take a picture and begin a scrapbook. Continue through the other members of the family. You may want to use a video camera to record different places and remember to tell stories about the person you're "visiting" as you go.

Or, your tour may take you across the state, the country or even abroad. You may take different grandchildren at different times or several at a time. It may not be possible to complete such a tour in one trip or two or even more. It may even take several years but it will be a wonderful family memoir and one which will live forever.

CHAPTER

16

CRUISES AND RANCHES

When you are traveling with two or more of your grandchildren you really may want to consider either a cruise or a dude ranch. Provided, that is, they provide enough activities to keep your little ones interested when they tire of you and vice versa.

If the prices paralyze you initially, consider that the costs listed include almost everything: transportation (cruises); food; care and entertainment. It also leaves time for you to do things which appeal to you (even if it is only relaxing on deck or under a tree with a good book) without feeling guilty.

CRUISES

If you have a trusted travel agent, check with her or him. If your usual agent can't help you, ask around and find one who specializes in cruise bookings and knows which cruise line offers what. Not all of them will answer your needs. After you have determined how much you want to spend and what type of cruise that amount will buy, start with questions such as:

- What type of programs are there for what ages? (If it's only sitting down and coloring all day, forget it
- What are the youngest and oldest ages for participation? What are the age divisions? (Nine year old Johnny won't go if three year old Jean is in the same place).
- How many counselors for how many children?
- Is there a library with children's books?
- How much space aboard ship is reserved for the children's activities?
- Is individual baby sitting available if Granny wants an evening of adult activities?
- Are pizzas, burgers and ice cream available throughout the day?
- Are there special menu choices for children in the main dining room?
- Is there a children's pool?
- Are there special hours for children in the main pools?
- Are swimming and/or snorkel lessons available?
- Is there a special movie theater for the kids? If not, will there be appropriate films shown at special times?
- Are there toys and games which can be checked out overnight?

If you find a cruise which you and your grand children truly like, you may want to consider it for an entire family reunion in the future. This can be a very special treat for all; grandparents, adult children and grandchildren.

RANCHES

Dude ranches, like cruises, can be the ideal spot for a whole family reunion especially if yours is an outdoor-loving family. There are activities for all ages so, no matter how many of you there are, pack up your cowboy gear (boots are an absolute must) and head west.

Although dude ranches have a great appeal for youngsters from 6 years up, teenagers seem to like them best. Many ranches have special teen counselors to take the kids on all-day outings. Being with your own age group is so important when one is in this in-between stage. The fact that you are willing to pay for a vacation, not insist that they spend every waking hour with you, and allow them to go off all day will greatly endear you to them. Be ready and eager to hear anything they want to share about their day. Listening is an art at which grandparents excel and being heard is something adolescents (like all of us) so need.

The following ranches specialize in children's programs:

Hunewill Circle H Guest Ranch
P.O. Box 368
Bridgeport, CA 93517
(619) 932-7933

Here, guests are assigned their own saddle horse during their stay. There are auto trips to deserted mining towns nearby in addition to a variety of other age appropriate activities.

Wilderness Trails Ranch
23486 Country Rd. 501
Bayfield, Colorado 81122
(970) 247-0722

Children from 6-12 can enjoy riding lessons, picnics, games and crafts. Teenagers and their counselors ride and hike; play volleyball and have hot tub parties.

Hidden Creek Ranch
7600 East Blue Lake Rd.
Harrison, Idaho 83833
(208) 689-3209

This ranch has trap shooting, archery, fly fishing, mountain hiking, evening activities and hay rides.

Lazy L & B Ranch
1072 E. Fork Rd.
Dubois, Wyoming 82513
(307) 455-2839

Children 5 and older participate in the programs here. There is even a supervised wrangler program where kids learn to rope and ride in safety. Other activities include swimming, fishing, riflery and horseshoes.

These ranches are only four of the dozens available. Check with a travel agent who has had experience in booking such vacations. Or, if you choose, visit the library or cruise the Internet then call the ranches directly until you are satisfied with your findings.

CHAPTER

17

VACATIONS WITH HANDICAPPED YOUNGSTERS

If you (as I do) have a seriously handicapped grandchild whom you want to take on a fun trip, take the following test before mentioning it to anyone:

- Am I physically and emotionally able to assume this responsibility?
- If a wheelchair is necessary, can I lift it in and out of the car, fold and unfold it and place my grandchild in it with ease? Do I know how to lock and unlock the wheels. If it isn't working right can I make minor adjustments? Do I know how to change the batteries?
- In case of G-Tube feeding, breathing exercises, diapering and/or other necessary routines, do I know the hows, wheres and whens? Will it exhaust me to carry them out regularly?

- Am I able to lift my youngster in and out of his or her daily bath?
- If the child is hearing impaired, do I sign well enough to be understood?
- Do I know when to assist my visually challenged child and when to allow independence?
- Can I accept the sympathetic stares and whispered comments of passersby with a smile on my face without trying to explain or defend?
- Are my coping skills adequate for any type of emergency which might arise?

Assuming you have considered these questions long and hard and your responses are in the affirmative, your next step is to broach your plan to the parents.

Ask for their honest opinions and advice. Do not, and I repeat, do not feel hurt or insulted if they totally negate the idea or subtly suggest it might be better if of one of them accompany you. Remember, they are not only are thinking of their child but also of you. Accept their suggestions and/or decisions with grace and appreciation.

You may not have thought of it, but taking one of the parents along could make the trip more pleasurable and relaxing for all. You could spend the same quality time with your grandchild and have help available if necessary. It also could give some valuable R and R to that parent.

If the word is "Go", your work has just begun. Planning, in this situation, is even more important than usually and needs to be started months in advance.

You are going to need to move in with your children and grandchild for whatever period of time is necessary for you to learn everything necessary for his or her care.

Once you, your young charge and his parents have chosen a destination, you need to start researching. Most travel books provide good, general information, but they can't be counted on for accessibility issues.

Write to the Chamber of Commerce in the area you plan to visit, tell them your plans, explain your problem and ask for their help. They should be able to give you access information and likely will refer you to disability organization in that city which may be of even greater help. The definition of accessibility may sometimes be in the eye of the beholder, even though the 1990 passage of the Americans With Disabilities Act has done much to streamline public awareness.

If you are flying, don't hesitate to ask the airline about its policies toward disabled traveler, e.g.:

- Will you be assisted in boarding?
- How about storing and/or transferring the wheelchair and its batteries (if any)?
- Can special dietary needs be met?
- How accessible are the bathrooms? (I have yet to see one which I believed to be adequate).

Try to find an airline which seems aware of disabilities and genuinely concerned for the comfort of its passengers.

Do your own research. Don't depend on a travel agent to find the airline or hotel for you. Travel agents are fine for booking reservations and securing tickets for the general population but not necessarily for the handicapped. If you really feel the need for an agent and don't know of one personally, call the National Tour Association (606) 226-4444 for a free listing of members who have had experience with disabled travelers.

When making hotel reservations, don't make them through the 800 number. Call the hotel directly and make sure the reservationist understands your specific needs. Do as you did with the airlines, ask questions. If you aren't satisfied with their answers, check with another hotel.

The same advice goes for car rental agencies.

Your choice of a destination will, of course, be guided, not only by your and your grandchild's interests, but also by the type and extent of his disability.

If you want to keep traveling to a minimum, you may consider renting a condominium at a beach. This can be great fun if your grandchild is ambulatory. Shell gathering, jumping in and out of the waves, building sand castles make for some fun times. *Attempting to push a wheelchair through the sand is not advised.*

On the Outer Banks in North Carolina there are several beaches with ramps and viewing platforms but the beaches themselves are soft and not accessible to regular wheelchair traffic. Many beaches have surf chairs which will roll over the sand. Check this out before you go.

Across the continent, San Diego's Mission Beach has a cement boardwalk and accessible walkway to the hard packed sand where your regular wheelchair can be pushed with ease.

Mountain vacations in a hotel alongside a cool, rocky stream with good, hard-packed mountain trails leading up to waterfalls, coves and glens to explore, wild flowers to study (you can't pick any in the National Parks) can be great for the wheelchair bound. The Great Smoky Mountain National Park is excellent for this. Write the Headquarters, 107 Park Headquarters Rd., Gatlinburg, TN 37738 for information.

Wonderful for your young history buffs, a trip to our nation's Capitol is essential. The Metro system in Washington is fully accessible. All stations have an elevator to and from the platform and a level surface from elevator to train. Tourmobile, (202) 554-7950, has vans with lifts and lock downs available with 24 hours notice. At the Smithsonian, the major spaces are accessible; guide dogs are allowed and visitors may request sign language, oral interpreters or touch tours with 10 days notice. Call (202) 786-2942.

Niagara Falls, Yellowstone National Park and Grand Canyon National Park are three of this nation's scenic wonders which are for the most part handicap accessible. Do contact the parks before you go for any special tips.

There is much in our larger cities which interests a youngster whose impairment is primarily physical. Problems can arise, though, when it comes to transportion to and from the airports. In New York City, for example, most express buses do not have wheelchair lifts and lockdowns. Gray Line Air Shuttle (with 48 hrs. notice) has minibuses with lifts and lock-downs and serves both LaGuardia and Newark Airports and the major hotels. Call (212) 757-6840. While more expensive than the express buses, it is considerably less than taxi cabs which will store collapsible wheelchairs and assist the users.

All Boston taxi companies have some accessible taxis with ramps and tie-downs. Two day notice is required. Call Boston Cabs (617) 536-5010 or Checker (617) 536-7000.

In Los Angeles, MTA has buses with lifts and lockdowns running between LAX and downtown hotels for $1.10, but finding transportation to the spread out places of interest is difficult and very pricey.

If you are considering Hawaii, write the Commission on Persons with Disabilities, 500 Ala Moana Blvd., Suite 210, Honolulu 96813 for their very complete guide.

Travelers with guide dogs should know that there is a law requiring a four month quarantine for all out-of-state service dogs.

DISNEY WORLD

As I mentioned earlier in this book, I normally do not consider an amusement or theme park when traveling with my grandchildren. I think this should be an adventure for a whole family, Mom, Dad and the kids. But there is an exception. There is no finer vacation spot to visit with a severely challenged grandchild than Florida's Disney World.

It is such a happy place, filled with beauty, laughter, music and color. The entire complex is handicapped accessible and the staff is trained to treat exceptional children as the special little people they are. My little Sarah was, indeed, given royal treatment.

Be sure to notify your hotel when you make reservations if you need wheelchair accessible accommodations or any other special needs. When you get to the Disney entrance you will be given a Handicapped permit to park in the designated zone near the entrance. From then on you will be delightfully assisted at every stop.

There are no waiting lines for you and your little Prince or Princess. Staff members will escort you to exit doors of the exhibits and rides and you will be whisked away to magic land. Many of the rides have special places for wheelchairs to be fastened down so your child can remain seated. Some others necessitate removal of the child from the chair to be seated or held by you on that particular vehicle. Aides are there to assist you and have the wheelchair waiting at the end of the ride.

You will find special, well-equipped feeding/changing stations at different places throughout the complex. And the storybook characters who stroll about the complex, hurry forward to shake hands, pose for pictures or give autographs to your youngster.

I cannot compliment the entire Disney World staff highly enough for their helpfulness, their anticipation of special needs and their kindness and consideration when dealing with special children. This applies to the Magic Kingdom, Epcot, MGM Studios and the hotels, not only within the Disney borders, but also in the surrounding area.

Regardless of where you go and what you do, remember to pace your fun. You have a fragile charge. So, go easy, relax, enjoy each other and have a wonderful time!

CHAPTER

18

WHAT TO DO ABOUT HOMESICKNESS AND OTHER PROBLEMS

No matter how well you plan and how bonded you are with your grandchild, problems can appear without warning. Darkness falls. The day is over. Tucked down in her hotel bed, Susie has visions of her home, her dog, her cat. Were they missing her? Did Mom remember to feed them? There is a big lump in her throat. it gets bigger and bigger. She can hardly breathe. Tears start.

What can Grandma do? Just what comes naturally. Put your arms around her, cuddle her closely, talk soothingly. Try to get her to tell you how she feels. Validate her feelings. Talking it out or getting involved in a new activity goes a long way to alleviate even the worst homesick attack. You might try puppet play or suggest she draw a picture of her family and pets.

If she can't or won't talk, a call home usually helps a lot and there is no rule that says there shouldn't be frequent calls back home if desired. If you get on the phone after she talks, you might speak glowingly of your plans for the next day. Hearing this and anticipating the fun of tomorrow may deter any more problems at that time.

In extreme cases where nothing works, ask her if she wants to go home tomorrow. She probably will say "yes", but by morning may have changed her mind. If she still wants to go home, take her. She just wasn't ready.

Older children may miss their friends as much as family and pets. Here, too, telephone calls can solve a lot. Most kids like to share their activities with a friend. It might be best for the grandparents to disappear for a little while to allow some telephone privacy.

If you are traveling one-on-one with a grandchild, your chances for a relatively peaceful time are greater. The dynamics are different. It is almost like you are best friends rather than grandparent-grandchild. You are sharing special things and laughing over silly little things which happened during the day.

Unless you are the exception and have absolute angels for grandkids, there will be some spats—probably tears—maybe even a tantrum along the way. Just relax, keep your cool. You have handled all this before. Nothing has changed that much since this youngster's parent was your child. Let her know that you know how she feels, but that sometimes it is impossible (dangerous, too expensive or whatever) to grant her every wish. The less you say the better. Listen if she wants to talk. Cut off the conversation if she wants to continue begging. Remind her that your no' means just that. Say it and hush.

When she begins to cool down you may suggest a new activity. A new adventure will make her forget her anger. Physical activity usually helps abate whining (a true irritant to most grandparents). A romp in the park, a hike around the hotel grounds or a swim in the pool expends some of that pent up energy and creates a more pleasant traveling companion.

If your grandchild becomes fearful of an activity, such as horseback riding or water rafting (even if it is something she wanted desperately to do), let her know no plans were etched in stone and it is okay to back out. If she wants to watch, fine. Chances are she will want to participate later. Never try to force a child into an activity against her will.

There may be a reason (at least in your grandchild's mind) to be fearful of a place. Perhaps you have just arrived in California and someone mentions earthquakes. She suddenly wants to go home. Sit down with her and explain that it is very doubtful if there will be an earthquake, but, if there were one, you are her grandparent, you love her very much and you will take care of her. That simple (and true) statement can give her the security she needs.

Adolescents are a different problem. They become bored easily and with boredom comes either complaining about everything or silent pouting. What to do? Think back to when you and he or she were planning the trip. Remember what it was he told you really interested him. You might tell him you wished you could find a place to do that activity (sailing, bike riding or whatever). Start thumbing through the Yellow Pages. It won't be long before he'll be trying to help you.

The problem, of course, is that this may not happen when you are in your hotel room. You may be in the car during a long driving day or on an airplane. After a brief contemplative silence, you might ask a thought provoking question—one which requires his or her considered opinion and an explanation (not just a yes or no answer). This can be the beginning of a real conversation and result in some intergenerational communication—thereby dispelling the boredom.

Rainy days at the beach (or anywhere else for that matter) can test any grandparent's creativity. This may be a good time to pull out that new travel game you were saving for such an emergency. Souvenir shopping, visiting a mall, or spending time in a toy store can make the time pass more quickly. Movies are great as are museums, if there are any around. It might pay you to drive some distance for either. By the time you come out, the sun may be shining.

Traveling with children always requires patience and flexibility. Be aware of their feelings. If they tend to be homesick or fearful, acknowledge these feelings. That will help the child cope with them. Stick, as much as possible, to familiar schedules. Always encourage your grandchildren to talk about anything which bothers them. Show how much you value and respect them.

Most of all, use your good common sense and let your love and joy in your grandchildren show through.

CHAPTER

19

CONCLUSION

The vacations discussed in this book have only scratched the surface of grandparent/grandchild travel possibilities. Hopefully it has stimulated your imagination and interest and will serve as a guide to planning your own wonderful trips.

Remember, if your budget is limited, your grandchildren young or you feel a little insecure, *stay close to home.*

Always try to find places to visit which are *child-friendly.*

And, no matter how many children you take, how much or little money you spend, keep the faith. *You are in for the adventure of a lifetime.*

So here's to all you travel-loving grandparents who want to share experiences and make life-long memories with your grandchildren. I bid you Bon Voyage!!

Pilot Books Reading Shelf

To order, simply call our toll-free number
(800) 79PILOT

Cheap Eats/Florida...4,000+ Places to Eat on a Budget by Phil Philcox. Florida's the birthplace of the early bird special and here's the book to help you avoid the worms. From the familiar fast-food chain to the mom and pop eatery, this comprehensive guide lists low-cost, conveniently located restaurants in every popular Florida tourist area. $9.95

Cruising Canada by Car...Good Times on a Budget by Virginia Spurlock. Take a trip to the foreign country next door. An experienced, enthusiastic and budget-conscious traveler takes you on a motor tour through Canada. An enjoyable read and handy guide. $8.95

The Doctor's Guide to Protecting Your Health Before, During, and After International Travel by W. Robert Lange, MD., Johns Hopkins Medical Institutions. Important pre-departure health planning; advice on health concerns; disease prevention; travel-related problems; climate and environmental safeguards; selected infectious disease risks; medical preparedness and assistance. Includes an essential checklist for senior travelers. $9.95

it's never too late to Understand and Enjoy Casino Gambling by Phil Philcox. Where to go for the most fun and what to do when you get there. Whether you're a seasoned gambler or just getting started, you'll feel like a pro when you've read this book. $8.95

1997/1998 Directory of Budget Motels (revised annually). Guide to the best in economy-priced chain motel accommodations in the United States and Canada. Motels meet rigid quality standards and are convenient to major highway systems. Includes motel headquarter listings for more information, many with toll free 800 numbers. $8.95

National Directory of Theme and Amusement Parks. Over 550 places to have fun! Arranged by state, this guide features senior citizen and children's discounts; admission fees and specifics on parks' rides; attractions and policy re one price for unlimited use of the facilities. $8.95